The Soul of a Soldier:

The True Story of a Mounted Pioneer in the Civil War

The Soul of a Soldier:

The True Story of a Mounted Pioneer in the Civil War

Myron M. Miller, great grandson of

Samuel K. Miller

March 2011

To order additional copies of this book, contact:
Xlibris Corporation
1-888-795-4274
www.Xlibris.com
Orders@Xlibris.com
94751

Contents

Acknowledgments

I would like to thank those persons and institutions that contributed significantly to the development of this book about my great-grandfather Samuel K. Miller.

First, a very special thanks to my cousin, Virginia Powers for serving as the editor of the book. We are both descended from this great-grandfather, and share our passion for the genealogy of the generations prior to Samuel K. Miller and those that have descended from him. Her insights, suggestions and perceptive eyes helped immensely in crafting the book. Even more importantly, she provided support to get me past obstacles and my frustrations at times when I faltered. She had considerable editing experience before she agreed to help me with this book, and that was a great asset to me throughout.

Second, my appreciation for all those in the Miller family who kept these letters in good shape from the time they were written during the Petersburg Campaign of 1864-1865. As a young man, I knew from my family that the letters existed, but had never seen them. Lydia Anna Miller, the widow of my cousin Kenneth Marcus Miller, told me in the early 1990s that she had provided the letters to the Crawford County Historical Society in Meadville, Pennsylvania.

Third, although he died in 1951, my great-uncle Milo H. Miller—one of the two sons of Samuel K. Miller—deserves credit for providing a record of important parts of Samuel's life. Milo was our family historian and wrote a book about the Miller family, entitled *A History and Genealogy of the Miller Family: 1725-1933,* and another about the Ellis family, entitled *A History and Genealogy of the Ellis Family: 1797-1935.*

Finally, my thanks to the staff of the Crawford County Historical Society in Meadville, Pennsylvania. They have kept the original letters securely since Lydia Anna Miller provided the letters in the late 1990s. The staff

9

helped me by copying the letters, and have been an excellent resource to me in providing me with research assistance in my genealogy work in that county. I am a member of that Society, for Crawford County was home to many of my ancestors going back to the mid-1800s.

My first visit to the town where Samuel K. Miller lived, Hartstown, Crawford County, Pennsylvania was when I was just four months old. I visited the village regularly with my parents until 1949, when both of my grandparents died. Because so many of my ancestors of the Miller and Ellis families are buried in the Hartstown Cemetery, I have continued to visit the town which was home to Samuel K. Miller and his family. I developed an acquaintance with the little town of my ancestors, and a caring for its people. In writing this book, it helped to have had so many years visiting Samuel's town.

Preface

Demetrius, an ancient Greek orator, literary critic, rhetorician and governor of Athens for ten years, once wrote: "Everyone reveals his own soul in his letters. In every other form of composition it is possible to discern the writer's character, but in none so clearly as the epistolary [the letters]." (Demetrius, *On Style, 227).*

Samuel K. Miller was my great-grandfather. Although he died almost 40 years before I arrived on this planet, I have come to know this man through the 46 letters he wrote during his nine months serving in the Union Army toward the end of the Civil War, most to his wife and several to one of his brothers-in-law who was also serving at that time.

Samuel Miller entered the 211th Infantry Regiment of the Union Army at Meadville, Pennsylvania on September 3, 1864 and was mustered out of the service at Alexandria, Virginia on June 2, 1865.

The letters from Samuel to his wife, Silence Miller, cover the time of his military service, the Petersburg Campaign. Samuel was not a young man when he joined the military, in fact, he was 42 years old. He left behind two young sons, my grandfather, Myron Manson Miller, age five years, and my great uncle Milo H. Miller, age one year. Although not a well-educated man, he was obviously self-educated, as evidenced by his letters. He had a maturity far beyond many of his fellow soldiers, and thus brought experience beyond what might have been expected of an enlisted man.

Before she passed away in 1996, I learned from Lydia Anna Miller, the wife of my cousin Kenneth Miller, that she had deposited the 46 letters at the Crawford County Historical Society in Meadville, Pennsylvania. With the help of the staff of that Society, those letters were located and copies made for me. I visited that Society on a wintry day in April 2001 and finally had a chance to see the letters that I knew had been kept by various family members since the end of the Civil War. What I found as I read those letters astounded me, for in those letters I had a very penetrating look into the mind and heart of my great-grandfather. I felt as though I had just opened a treasure chest! The more I read, the more I realized that those letters provided a look into the whole man, into his soul.

From Samuel's letters, written during the intense crucible of war, emerges a portrait of a man of high principles and ideals who shared in these letters to his wife his everyday experiences as a soldier as well as his struggles to become "a better Christian." Samuel was dedicated to serving his country and his fellow man. Through his correspondence during the nine months of service, he continued to be involved with a broad array of family members across several states.

That initial reading of Samuel's letters motivated me to write this book, for several reasons. First, I felt a responsibility to capture for me, for my extended family and for those who will follow me in future generations, the values and ideals of the Miller family that came through in those letters. I have admired the descendants of Samuel Miller whom I have known personally; his sons and their families, his grandsons and their families. I have respected them for their laudable values, their dedication to serve their families and their fellow man, and their service to their country. Here, in Samuel's letters, I saw the essence of those excellent values. I wanted to capture those values and the essence of our souls for my sake, for my family and for others who may be motivated to search for their values and ideals in the history of their families. I will endeavor at this stage of my life to live the values I saw in Samuel's letters, and I hope that my descendants will also be motivated to live those values; strong personal faith, dedication to their families and service to others, particularly those in need.

The letters cried out to me that Samuel's story must be told and shared. I thought that if I did not tell his story, it would never be told. In addition to sharing the letters with all who might find them interesting, I wanted to use my own voice to organize the essence of these letters, not just in chronological order but also in ways that would highlight the character and values of Samuel K. Miller.

My second motivation for writing this book is to trace the effect that Samuel's wartime experience had on his Christian faith. His letters portray a man who, on reflection, was not a dedicated Christian before entering the service. His letters show his willingness to study the Bible, his struggle to become a better Christian, and, finally, a commitment to be a much more involved and committed Christian upon his return home.

Thirdly, I felt that his role as a "Mounted Pioneer" was somewhat distinctive, and that his description of the daily life and his placement in times of combat was a story unto itself. Samuel was selected from his initial service as an infantryman in the 211th Pennsylvania Volunteers Regiment to be a Mounted Pioneer in the Headquarters Ninth Army Corps of the Union Army. This 25 man unit was removed from the location of the battles so they would always be available for building and repairing roads, railroads and other types of construction. Samuel had had extensive experience as a cabinet and furniture maker, as well as in bridge building and other construction before entering the army. That assignment not only suited Samuel's skills, but also virtually ensured his survival. Samuel's descriptions of that rather selective role provide a unique insight not usually found in Civil War chronicles.

Samuel entered the Civil War several months after the beginning of the ten month long Petersburg campaign that ended in April 1865. Concerning the importance of that campaign, Noah Andre Trudeau stated in his book *The Last Citadel:*

> *"No campaign of the Civil War equaled the siege of Petersburg, Virginia. Petersburg was the object of the longest military action ever waged against an American city. More battles were fought and more lives lost in its defense than over any of the other, better known Southern citadels: Richmond, Atlanta and Vicksburg."*

> *For 292 days one of the great dramas of the Civil War played out over the fate of the city that historian Fletcher Pratt called 'the last bulwark of the Confederacy.' 'Petersburg . . .,' wrote Richard J. Sommers, was the 'guardian of Richmond's lifeline to the Southern heartland.' Through it channeled supply lines vital to the Confederate capital. Without Petersburg, Richmond was doomed: it was that simple. Ulysses*

S. Grant wanted Petersburg; Robert E. Lee was equally determined that it would not succumb." (Trudeau, xi)

Excellent books have been written about the Petersburg campaign, so this is not meant to be another. Rather, it is about one soldier involved in that campaign, his experiences, and what effects they had on him and his family.

Samuel's decision to enlist in the Civil War came just 14 months after his wife's brother, Philander Coburn Ellis, a soldier with the First Minnesota, had been killed at Gettysburg on July 3, 1863. Silence also had three other brothers serving in the Union Army, two in Pennsylvania regiments and one in a Michigan regiment. One can only imagine Silence's emotions as Samuel, too, was leaving her and the two children to join the battle.

Sadly, we do not have copies of the letters from Silence to Samuel. Those letters were destroyed by Samuel, who did not want those letters to fall into the hands of others, should he die. However, we learn a lot about her from Samuel's letters, since he often answered her questions or comments on various aspects of her life at home as well as his living arrangements, his dedication to worship, etc.

I have studied the Civil War and have visited the battlefields where Samuel fought and served. It is possible to connect his experiences with the chronicles of various battles and to visualize the setting for his experiences and observations. These letters, saved since 1865, are treasures of information about Samuel's unique experiences in the Civil War. Having read those letters, I believe that Samuel K. Miller's story deserves to be added to the rich records of that terrible conflict. The letters provide a chronology of his service with the 211th Pennsylvania Volunteer Infantry and the Mounted Pioneer Corps attached to the Union Ninth Corps. More than just the chronology, however, these letters portray the mind and soul of this man.

This book is an endeavor to capture the essence of Samuel Miller's journey through the final year of the Civil War, so that we might have a deeper understanding of the type of transformation that bloody conflict imposes on one's whole being. I have endeavored to capture that "inner man,"—the *soul* of the man—so that the experiences of this one man allow us to learn more about the transformation of men in the midst of a war.

Because he wrote 46 rather extensive letters, we can get to know Samuel very well. He opened his mind and heart to his wife and to other family members. But, what is the soul, and why examine the soul of a soldier?

Why the "*soul*" of a *soldier?* Webster's New World Dictionary provides several definitions of "soul."

> *"an entity which is regarded as being the immortal or spiritual part of a person and though having no physical or material reality, is credited with the functions of thinking and willing, and hence determining all behavior."*

> *"the moral and emotional nature of a human being."*

> *"spiritual or emotional warmth, force, etc., or evidence of this."*

In his book *War and the Soul,* Edward Tick wrote extensively about what happens to one's soul in wartime. He has dealt extensively with those suffering from PTSD (Post Traumatic Stress Syndrome) and made this observation:

> *. . .The common therapeutic model . . . misses the point that PTSD is primarily a moral, spiritual and aesthetic disorder—in effect, not a psychological but a soul disorder. All of its [PTSD] aspects concern dimensions of the soul, inasmuch as the soul is the part of us that responds to morality, spirituality, aesthetics and intimacy. Such aspects can be healed only by strategies aimed at them directly in this context . . . . Almost all cultures and spiritual traditions of the world have had some concept of the soul and the means for preserving its well-being. However, in our scientific and technological era, soul is not a popular concept. "Post-traumatic stress disorder is our modern metaphor for the condition of soul sickness; the quasi-scientific name allows us to find a place for it among the psychological categories we use today to analyze the human experience.* (Tick 108)

According to Edward Tick, "Socrates taught that the soul is that which distinguishes good from evil; it is improved by choosing good and harmed by choosing evil." (Ibid 110)

What happened to the "moral and emotional nature," the "spiritual part of a person," of Samuel Miller during his year in the midst of the Civil War?

The ultimate expression of how the experience affected him was captured in one of his last letters, where he said:

> *I feel happy to think that the war is at a close. I also feel sad and shed tears to read about those poor rebels and blacks—how rejoiced they are to be liberated from bondage. The playing of a band of musicians makes me shed tears. It seems that my heart is completely broken. The boys all say that I am so quiet. I cannot help it. I feel so.*

Samuel had suffered no physical wounds, but his soul was deeply wounded.

Yet from this sadness, Samuel returned to civilian life and became an esteemed citizen of his town of Hartstown and of Crawford County, Pennsylvania. Perhaps Samuel found deeper meaning in serving his family and community precisely because of his wartime experiences. I am reminded of a portion of a passage from Kahlil Gibran's "The Prophet," which says:

> *"The deeper that sorrow carves into your being, the more joy you can contain."*

Although he may have suffered wounds to his soul during the time he served in the Civil War, as shown many times in his letters, we can infer from the nature of his return to civilian life that he was able to heal from those wounds reasonably soon. Very quickly he was caring for his wife and two small boys, tending his sizable vegetable garden, his cabinet-making, and even moving into a prominent role in the community as the undertaker of the village. It is likely that because Crawford County, and specifically the town of Hartstown, predominantly favored the saving of the Union, he would have been welcomed rather warmly back into the community.

Samuel was guided by his soul, by his integrity. Heraclitus (c. 544 B.C.-c. 483 B.C., Greek philosopher) stated it well:

"The soul is dyed the color of its thoughts. Think only on those things that are in line with your principles and can bear the light of day. The content of your character is your choice. Day by day, what you do is who you become. Your integrity is your destiny—it is the light that guides your way."

Samuel's life served as a model for his two sons, both of whom lived lives of service; to his grandchildren, several of whom served in the military in World War I; to a great-grandson who served in the U.S. Navy in World War II; and to me as I served in the U.S. Army 1956-1958. May the inspiration continue to flow from his letters to anyone who is committed to serve his fellow man, whether it be in the military, in education, in church and missions service, in their work, or in many other countless ways.

In his book, *"The World According to Mr. Rogers: Important Things to Remember,"* Hyperion. 2003,. Fred Rogers, educator, minister, and TV host of *"Mr. Rogers' Neighborhood,"* made this statement:

"Each generation, in its turn, is a link between all that has gone before and all that comes after. That is true genetically, and it is equally true in the transmission of identity. Our parents gave us what they were able to give, and we took what we could of it and made it a part of ourselves. If we knew our grandparents, and even our great-grandparents, we will have taken from them what they could offer to us, too. All that helps to make us who we are. We in our turn, will offer what we can of ourselves to our children and their offspring."

"Grandparents are both our past and our future. In some ways, they are what has gone before, and in others they are what we will become."

It is my hope that my own family, for this generation and generations to come, will know more about their own roots, the people who preceded them in this life journey. While this is not a story of nobility, it is a story of one of thousands of individual common people who have been models of a free, passionate people. I am honored to be the one to bring this story to my family, and to all those interested in finding new dimensions of the human spirit.

A note to the reader. Samuel's letters are included chronologically in the appendix. Throughout the chapters of this book, I will indicate which letter the quote came from: #4 means that the quote came from the fourth of the 46 letters.

Chapter 1

Return Home

"Silence, the war is coming to a close fast . . . . Keep in good cheer. We shall soon see each other again, if not until the expiration of my year that is fast wasting away. Fret not about me. I will take care of myself, also of my Soul." (Excerpt from a letter by Samuel K. Miller to his wife, whose name was Silence, on January 24, 1865.)

At about midnight on June 6, 1865, Samuel K. Miller stepped off the train near his home at the small village of Atlantic, Pennsylvania, having boarded the train several hours earlier at Camp Reynolds, near Pittsburgh. That was the end of the journey that had started on September 2, 1864, when he volunteered to join the Union Army as part of Company A, 211th Pennsylvania, mustered into the service at Meadville, Pennsylvania. Samuel had entered the Union Army as a forty-two year old cabinet maker, and as a private. He was mustered out of the service in Alexandria, Virginia on June 2, 1865.

Surely no one was there to meet him as he got off the train into the cool night air, typical of early June in Northwestern Pennsylvania. It is very likely that everyone in the village was asleep.

Samuel set off on the long walk with thoughts swirling through his head about his family, about the community to which he was returning, and the experiences of those recent months in the Petersburg campaign. In his mind's eye, he could still visualize the violence, the battles, the friends he had made, and the occasional periods of boredom. He found his way in the darkness along a road that he knew instinctively to his home in Hartstown, another small town in Crawford County, Pennsylvania. A walk of five miles, with his few modest belongings, was not very far compared to the marches he had endured during the

Petersburg Campaign. On one occasion he had carried a knapsack and haversack with four days rations and harness and guns, weighing about eighty pounds. That march had covered forty-four miles in twenty-four hours.

He thought of the home to which he was returning after being away for nine life-changing months: his wife, who had the interesting first name of Silence; a six year old boy, Myron (my grandfather), and a two year old son, Milo (my great uncle). He had missed them very much, though Silence did her best through frequent letters to keep Samuel close to her and the children. Still, at those young ages, nine months makes a big difference in the size and behavior of children, and Samuel could only speculate about how much they had grown and changed.

He would have felt wonderful about being home again, but he would also have realized the need to get on with life and get to work providing for his family. He had received a $500 bounty for volunteering as part of the Turnerville quota in Crawford County, Pennsylvania. Quotas had been assigned geographically as a means of gaining volunteers; only if the quotas were not filled would men be drafted from that area. Samuel's bounty had been deposited in the general store in Hartstown, from which Silence was to draw provisions for the family while Samuel was away. That $500 was partially gone, so he would need to get back to his cabinet making and growing the vegetables in his garden that provided for the family throughout the year.

He would have wondered about the feelings of the people of Hartstown now that the war had ended, for some had been either anti-war, or ambivalent about the Civil War. Those who were ambivalent felt little concern whether or not the South were to separate and establish a separate country. Some were strongly anti-Lincoln. Hartstown was far removed physically from the battles, but the people were well-informed about the details of the war despite the distance.

Samuel, having volunteered, had expressed rather angry feelings in the letters he had written to his wife about some of the men in the community who hadn't served, but now it was time to engage with those people again. With that small population, one would see just about everyone in the community every day. He wondered how he would feel about the people. Would he feel resentment toward some of those fellows—and even the ladies—or would he feel so relieved to be back home safely that he would put all of the negative feelings behind him?

The memories of his months at or near the front in Petersburg would haunt him for the rest of his days. He could still see the two deserters hung before 13,000 men; the amputated arms and legs after a major battle, and countless other scenes, now so distant. He had been taken away from his regiment in December 1864 and reassigned to the Mounted Pioneer Corps, a twenty-five man unit that would now be considered engineers, attached to the Headquarters Ninth Army Corps. Those men were drawn from several Pennsylvania regiments. His unit provided a vital service building roads, bridges, hospitals and repairing them. To perform these tasks, Samuel had been issued an ax and a horse. Why had he been chosen for duty as a Mounted Pioneer? In his letters to Silence, Samuel speculated that he had been chosen for that assignment because of his maturity and his cabinet making skills.

From his arrival near Petersburg in September 1864 until this reassignment in December, he had had some harrowing experiences, and even after he became a Mounted Pioneer he was never far from the heart of the battles with that twenty-five man unit. Nevertheless, it is possible that this reassignment may have saved his life during the long months of the bloody Petersburg campaign. Was this luck? Providence?

With all the thoughts pertaining to the outward aspects of his life, what was he thinking—more importantly—regarding the inward aspects of his life? The experiences he described in his letters to Silence surely had changed his inner being. He had become a much stronger Christian during the nine months away, so it would be a contradiction if he were to live as a more dedicated Christian and continue to be antagonistic toward his neighbors. How would he feel about the Copperheads, that faction of Democrats who opposed the Civil War and wanted an immediate peace settlement with the Confederates? About those in the community who were hostile to Silence because of her abolitionist leanings? Would he and his friends and neighbors be able to put past differences aside and resume their daily lives without rancor? In these and in all aspects of his life, how would he "take care of his soul" as he had indicated in his letter to Silence in January 1865?

Samuel had survived. During the last days of the war, his unit had gone through Richmond and as far as Burkesville, near Appomattox, by April 9. From there he had been sent back to City Point then Alexandria, Virginia, where he was mustered out of the service on June 2, 1865. Now, each step Samuel took was taking him closer to Hartstown and home.

Silence knew from his most recent letter that he would be arriving home soon. She also knew that he was uninjured and well. However, she did not know exactly when to expect him. Would she be shocked to hear him at the door in the wee hours of the morning? He had told her not to expect him until she heard the gate close and his whistle! Would she wake the boys to see their daddy? The last nine months had often seemed like an eternity, but now he was walking on the road he knew so well—he had walked it hundreds of times—but this time it was so different.

Chapter 2

Who Was This Soldier—Samuel K. Miller?

Samuel Miller was born May 14, 1822 at McSherrystown, Adams County, Pennsylvania, the next to youngest of nine children in the family. His parents were John Miller and Elizabeth Shriver. Elizabeth was a member of the large and well-known Shriver family residing in Adams County, Pennsylvania and also Maryland.

John Miller and Elizabeth Shriver were married in Adams County on July 4, 1803, the same day the Louisiana Purchase was signed. About 1813, John Miller sold the family home and his 252 acre farm in what is now Carroll County, Maryland, and moved to Adams County, Pennsylvania. By 1814, John Miller was operating a general store which provided a broad range of essential home goods for the local community of Mt. Pleasant. John Miller also sold liquor there, and the establishment was sometimes referred to as a "tavern and house of public entertainment." According to records from that period the store was located near the McSherrystown to York-Gettysburg Turnpike.

John Miller needed references from a number of local business people who would vouch for his integrity, and those handwritten letters show a list of some of the well-known names in that locale; Andrew Shriver, John Hinkle, and Adam Eichelberger. The first petition was signed in 1814, and last petition was signed April 16, 1823. The original handwritten license renewal applications are in the file of the Adams County Historical Society in Gettysburg, Pennsylvania.

In addition to managing the general store, John Miller was a wagoner on the National Pike, approximately along what is US Route 40 today, delivering goods from Baltimore to the Pittsburgh area, and then on to Cleveland. His wife and children were left to operate the tavern and general store while he was transporting his load over the mountains in huge Conestoga wagons that were drawn by four, six or eight-horse teams. Salt was one of the most important commodities that he carried in his wagon. As soon as the weather permitted in the spring, he left his home to tend to this business.

On one of John Miller's trips to Cleveland in 1823, he stopped in Springfield Township near Petersburg, Ohio. There he spent the night with an old friend, Jacob Musser, who had earlier moved from Adams County, Pennsylvania, to this easternmost part of Ohio. Jacob Musser owned a farm in the Petersburg area and was willing to sell part of his land. By that time, John Miller was weary of the life of a wagoner and decided to move to that new territory which had just opened to expansion in the early 1800s. The two men struck a deal for John Miller to purchase 200 acres of land adjacent to the Pennsylvania state line. The purchase price was $500 in cash, plus John's wagon, horses, and harnesses.

While the family in McSherrystown was operating the tavern and general store, John Miller proceeded to build a saw and grist mill on the 200 acres he had purchased in Petersburg, Ohio. He built a dam across the creek at the lower level of his property to supply the power needed to power the mill. By having both the grist mill and saw mill, he was able to keep the mill productive most of the year. He also made whiskey and "cherry bounce," a mixture of wild cherries, whiskey, sugar and water, steeped for about three months. Later, in 1823, the family moved from Pennsylvania to their new home in Petersburg, Ohio.

As a young boy in Petersburg, Ohio, Samuel was kept busy running errands for his father and older brothers. When he was old enough, he attended the village school in Petersburg, and he was taught for many years by an old German schoolmaster by the name of Philip Swisher.

> *Well did he remember his teacher and the school in the village and ever afterwards loved to tell of his school days when he learned reading, writing, arithmetic . . . . Some forty or fifty boys and girls of all ages from six to twenty-one sat on hard wooden benches from nine till four . . . . Samuel attended school until he was twenty years old.* (Miller, *Miller Family*, 108)

Managing such a wide variety of children and young people, while teaching a wide variety of subjects, surely took the skills of a master. Philip Swisher selected Samuel for a very special task, making quill pens for the younger students after Samuel had finished his "sums," his mathematics assignments.

> *He retained the love and respect of his old master as long as the latter lived and always revered his memory. The days spent at the village school were his only opportunity to secure an education, but he improved them well and obtained a good knowledge of the common branches of education . . . . He was a reader of current history and politics all his life and took great interest in educational matters.* (Miller, *Miller Family* 109)

Peter Swisher not only taught Samuel the subjects he needed for his future work, but also inspired him to be a lifelong learner, an attribute that has been handed down through subsequent generations of the Miller family. Samuel, with his wife Silence, named their two boys after two outstanding men from the golden days of ancient Greece, Myron and Milo of Croton. The choice of names for the two sons indicates the special interest that Samuel had in history. We can also infer that Mr. Swisher put significant emphasis on handwriting because of the legibility of Samuel's letters. Whatever else was taught in those one-room village schoolhouses, they produced students capable of very good handwriting. Students in those days took great pride in their handwriting.

As he neared the end of his schooling, Samuel became involved in helping David, one of his older brothers, in his work as a drover. A drover was a person who "drove" cattle and sheep from the farms to the market, and David and Samuel drove cattle and sheep from Ohio across the fields to markets in Pennsylvania.

One of Samuel's duties was to watch over the sheep and keep them from nibbling the mountain laurel along the sides of the roads in the mountainous areas. The mountain laurel could have disastrous effects on the sheep, and was referred to as "lamb kill." The drovers spent their nights at wayside taverns where there might be thirty or forty six-horse teams in the wagon yard. Near the tavern was a large lot that would have been a sight to behold:

> *. . . one hundred Kentucky mules, one thousand hogs in another enclosure, and as many fat cattle from the rich valleys of Ohio and Indiana in adjacent fields. The music made by this large number of hogs, in eating corn on a frosty night, he [Samuel] could never forget. He had seen as many as four thousand head of cattle headquartered at one place in a single night.* (Miller, *Miller Family*, 116)

In the evenings after the drovers had eaten and fed their herds, they would gather with the other drovers and have a rather festive time. They shared stories of what had happened that day and sang. On occasion, someone played a violin so the drovers could have a "hoe-down." After the festivities of the night, they brought out their beds, settled on the floor near the fireplace and slept soundly from their day of work and evening of pleasure. The following morning they would be up at the daybreak to feed their herds and organize the cattle and sheep into droves for the next days' travel. Typically they traveled about twelve miles each day.

It may be hard to imagine the space required to move thousands of cattle or sheep, particularly since one drover didn't have the road to himself. Samuel provided this description to his son Milo H. Miller:

> *The National Road was sufficiently wide to permit a twenty-five foot strip on each side of the carriageway, which was sixteen feet wide. This twenty-five foot space provided plenty of room for the many thousands of cattle, horses, sheep and hogs driven along the highway.* (Miller, *Miller Family* 116)

On some of their stopovers during the journey, they stayed at taverns. Samuel mentioned the "old Red Lion Hotel" in Pittsburgh, Pennsylvania as being a particular favorite. As they passed through Pittsburgh, the drovers had another interesting form of entertainment. There they encountered raftsmen who worked on the Allegheny River. They got into fights, for it seems that there was some particular grudge that the two groups had for each other.

When David and Samuel finished the journey with their herds, they might obtain an occasional ride on a horse during the long trek home, but for the most part, they walked. Hardy souls, those drovers!

In addition to his work as a drover, and while still attending school in Petersburg, Samuel began to learn the cabinet-making trade. When he was about eighteen years old, he began a three-year apprenticeship with John Hayes of Petersburg. When he finished his apprenticeship, Samuel went into business for himself. He started his business in Sydney, Ohio, then moved on to Bowling Green, Ohio. As a diversion from cabinet-making, he worked for a while in the lead mines in Galena, Illinois. During this time, the 1840s, many people were moving to the Northwest, to states such as Illinois, Wisconsin and Minnesota. Samuel joined the migration to the frontier, travelling up the Mississippi River to St. Paul, Minnesota, where he stayed for two years, during which time he voted for the admission of the state to the Union.

It is quite likely that during his travel and work, Samuel not only practiced his cabinetry, but also used his woodworking skills in construction projects such as the building and repairing of bridges. Later, during his service in the Union Army, these skills would prove to be very valuable.

In 1856, Samuel left Minnesota and moved to Adamsville, Crawford County, Pennsylvania to live with his sister Elizabeth. She had married Loring Mayo and moved from Petersburg, Ohio to Adamsville. There Samuel established his cabinetry trade. While living with his sister in Adamsville, Samuel met Silence Ford Ellis, the daughter of John and Susan Ann (Ford) Ellis of Hartstown, also in Crawford County, Pennsylvania. Silence had moved with her family from Mayfield, Maine in 1841.

Samuel and Silence were married in Adamsville on January 29, 1857 and established a home in East Fallowfield Township, Crawford County, Pennsylvania. Samuel purchased five acres of land from his father-in-law, John Ellis, set up a shop and began his carpentry trade.

Myron Manson Miller, my grandfather, was born to Samuel and Silence on Washington's birthday, February 22, 1859. Their second child, Milo Meade Miller was born September 4, 1863. Milo later dropped Meade and just inserted the letter "H," since he did not want to be another MMM like his brother. Like so many self-sufficient people in this era, Samuel raised vegetables and owned a few farm animals in order to supply his family with some of the necessities of life. Some years later, Milo Miller said that the years from 1859 to 1869 were especially happy years for Samuel, even though it was interrupted by his service in the Union Army, starting in September 1864.

With his wife Silence, Samuel was a member of the Free Will Baptist Church in Adamsville, Pennsylvania. He had been born into a Lutheran family in 1822 in Adams County, Pennsylvania. There is no record of his church membership during his years in Petersburg, Springfield Township, now Mahoning County, Ohio, nor is there a record of his church attendance for the years during his travels to the upper Midwest. The possible influence of his membership in the Free Will Baptist Church will be addressed in Chapter 16, "Growth in Faith."

Chapter 3

Background of the Ellis Family and Their Sacrifices During the Civil War: The Death of Philander Coburn Ellis of the 1st Minnesota

Silence Ford Ellis, now Silence Miller, Samuel's wife, was the youngest of a family of ten children. Silence's mother, Susan Ann (Ford) Ellis, was living in Hartstown, Pennsylvania, near Samuel and Silence. It was in Hartstown that Samuel and Silence had met and were married in 1857. On a trip to the family home in Maine in October 1862, Susan's husband John Ellis, became ill and died within a matter of a few days. Heartsick, Susan buried her husband at Greenville, Maine, then returned to Hartstown.

It is very likely that John and Susan Ellis had been abolitionists. A notation in his obituary stated: "He [John] was an uncompromising friend of the slave." In addition, John and Susan had named one of their sons Lorenzo Dow Ellis after one of the most famous abolitionists of that era. In his book, *Lorenzo Dow*, Benajmin Brawley describes this well-known abolitionist and his strong views regarding slavery.

> *This is the record of a remarkable and eccentric white man who devoted himself to a life of singular labor and self denial. In any consideration of the South one could not avoid giving at least passing notice to Lorenzo Dow as the foremost itinerant preacher of his time, as the first Protestant who expounded the gospel in Alabama and Mississippi, and as reformer who at the very moment when cotton was beginning to be supreme, presumed to tell the South that slavery was wrong.* (Brawley 265)

As a result, this liberal-minded man was naturally opposed to slavery. He was as outspoken a champion of freedom as lived in America in his day. "Slavery in the South," said he, "is an evil that calls for national reform and repentance." He thought that this "national scourge in this world," might be antidoted before the storm "gathered and burst." (Ibid.)

John and Susan Ellis may have heard Lorenzo Dow speak and been influenced by him during his extensive travels in New England. Could they have been involved in the Underground Railroad during the time they lived in Mayfield, Maine? That is speculation and remains for future researchers to investigate. Nevertheless, John and Susan may have imparted their attitude of being "an uncompromising friend toward the slaves" to their children. In fact, Samuel refers to Silence as "an abolitionist wife" in one of the letters he wrote to her during the Civil War.

While a belief in abolition may not have been stated as a reason for joining the Union Army by any of the Ellis boys, it may have shaped their attitudes as they served. Silence may have been able to cope with the absence of Samuel if she thought that his service might result in the abolishment of slavery. Again, that is speculation, for the letters, while mentioning Silence being "an abolitionist wife," make rather little of the slavery issue, and abolition is never discussed as such.

At one time, Silence's parents, John and Susan Ellis, had four sons in the Union Army. Two of the sons, Benjamin and Enoch, became members of the same company. They were quite fortunate, as Milo H. Miller describes their experience.

They [Benjamin and Enoch] were mustered into the service August 30, 1862 at Camp Curtin, Harrisburg, Pennsylvania . . . . The brothers were in Lincoln's body guard until the end of the war. They were mustered out June 15, 1865.

The 150th Regiment of Pennsylvania, Volunteer Infantry, proceeded to Washington and was immediately assigned to guard duty in and about the city. Company K, in which Ben and Enoch served, was stationed at the Soldiers Home, the summer residence of the President. This company continued to act as the President's body guard until after the assassination of Mr. Lincoln. (Miller, *Ellis Family* 9)

It is interesting to note that four other men from the little town of Hartstown were also assigned to that body guard unit.

President Lincoln divided his time between the Soldier's Home and the White House. The Soldier's Home was about three miles north of the White House and in a somewhat cooler part of the city of Washington, D.C. President Lincoln and his family lived in the "President's Cottage" adjacent to the main building of the Soldiers Home during the summer months and in the White House during the winter. The duty of Company K of the 150th Pennsylvania Regiment was to keep guard of the President's home night and day. The commander of Company K, Captain Dickerson, accompanied the President to and from the White House every day. Periodically, Captain Dickerson had breakfast or dinner with the President, and the soldiers in Company K were in such close contact with the Lincoln's that they came to be considered to be part of the President's family.

At one point, after the 150th suffered great losses in the War, there was a call for Company K to join the rest of their regiment. Despite that pressure, President Lincoln chose to have Company K stay with him, since he felt that that Captain Derickson and his soldiers had performed so well. As a result, the company remained on duty throughout the year, both summer and winter, until their term of enlistment ran out June 15, 1865. (Bates 656-658).

Fortunately, the assignment to guard President Lincoln kept Benjamin and Enoch from the intense battles fought by the rest of the 150th Regiment. One can only imagine their grief when Lincoln was assassinated, for they most likely would have been in his presence shortly before that fatal night. Were any of the soldiers in Company K assigned to guard Mr. Lincoln that evening?

On September 6, 1861 John and Susan Ellis' third son, Nathan Ford Ellis, enlisted in the Second Cavalry Regiment of Michigan, a unit that later was engaged in some very significant battles of the Civil War. Nathan served until being honorably discharged as a corporal at

Cincinnati, Ohio on January 6, 1863. When he enlisted, Nathan was a member of the senior class at Hillsdale College in Michigan. Hillsdale College was initially established in 1844 by the Free Will Baptist Church which strongly opposed slavery. It is likely that Nathan chose to attend Hillsdale College because he and his family were members of that church.

> *Though established by Freewill Baptists, Hillsdale has been officially non-denominational since its inception. It was the first American College to prohibit in its charter any discrimination based on race, religion or sex, and became an early force for the abolition of slavery. It was also only the second college in the nation to grant four-year liberal arts degrees to women. (www.hillsdale.edu)*

With this mission, it is not surprising that many of the men at Hillsdale College would enter the Union Army very early in the conflict.

> *A higher percentage of Hillsdale students enlisted during the Civil War than from any other western college. Of the more than 400 who fought for the Union, four won the Congressional Medal of Honor, three became generals and many more served as regimental commanders. Sixty gave their lives.*

> *Because of the College's anti-slavery reputation and its role in founding the new Republican party (Professor Edmund Fairfield was a leader at the first convention), many notable speakers visited its campus during the Civil War era, including Frederick Douglass and Edward Everett, who preceded Lincoln at Gettysburg. (www.hillsdale.edu)*

The three sons, Benjamin, Enoch and Nathan survived their experiences in the Civil War, but a fourth brother was not so fortunate. After the loss of her husband, who had died in October 1862, Susan faced another tragedy in July 1863. Cobe was killed in the battle of Gettysburg.

Susan's son, Silence's brother, Philander Coburn Ellis, known by his friends as "Cobe," had joined the First Minnesota at Fort Snelling on April 29, 1861. He had gone to Minnesota because of the promise of good work in the lumber regions. Cobe's unit was among the first to answer President Lincoln's call for 75,000 troops to put down the rebellion of the South.

Cobe was wounded and taken prisoner at the Battle of Bull Run on July 21, 1861. He was taken to a Confederate hospital in Richmond, Virginia, then later sent to Jefferson Barracks near St. Louis, paroled, sent home for a furlough and then returned to his command on December 22, 1862. He served again with the First Minnesota in time to take part in the battle of Gettysburg six months later.

Cobe was killed during the charge on the enemy's lines on the evening of July 2, 1863. The First Minnesota was sent as a shock force against the charging Confederates after the defeat of Sickle's Third Army Corps at the Peach Orchard. That charge by the First Minnesota saved the center of the Union Army line, but it was accomplished at a terrible cost. Out of the 262 men that went into action, only 47 returned, leaving 215 dead or wounded. (Miller, *Ellis Family* 56)

One can only imagine Susan Ellis' grief as she read the letter that Cobe's tent mate, S. O. Seymour, wrote to her. At times Seymour refers to Cobe as "Philo" or just "Ellis:"

> *Camp near Hagerstown, Maryland Hartstown, Pa.   Mrs. S.A. Ellis*
> *July 11, 1863*
>
> *Dear Madam,*
>
> *P.C. Ellis was fighting for his country and doing his duty like a good soldier and an honorable man. He was my tent mate ever since he came back to the army, and a better man or a kinder-hearted, quiet, good companion I never expect to find. He is at rest. He was shot through the head on the charge made by our regiment on the enemy's line on the evening of the 2ⁿᵈ of July near Gettysburg, Pa. He never knew he was hurt. Our losses were severe ******** (At this point the letter is folded and cannot be deciphered) and three companies were not in the fight, only 92 left after the fight. I found him on the way back to the lines a short time after the charge but he was dead. He was my dearest friend. I felt lonely. We buried him decently and marked his*

grave. He was the first one laid in one large grave near a large oak tree on the field. I saved his wallet and some few papers. All the rest was lost. I lost all my things while attending to the wounded, and have had no chance to write since, for we have been following the enemy and now are before them, in line of battle. We expect a hard battle tonight or in the morning. There were only five men and one sergeant left in our Company that went into the battle on the 2ⁿᵈ of July. How many will be left after this fight who can tell, but we fight a just and good cause, and feel willing to die like men if that be our fate, or bear with the pain of the wounds if wounded.

We have had some very hard marches since the battles near Gettysburg and I almost wish sometimes I had poor Philo's place. Then all would be at peace. Daniel Weaver, our other tent mate, was wounded in the right knee but not dangerously. I expect he has written to some of Ellis' friends. I opened this letter (the last one written to P.C. Ellis by his mother on June 16, 1863) to get your address and this is all the paper I have or can get now. The first opportunity I will give you more particulars. Ellis fought like a man, always did his duty, and died as a soldier wishes to die when his time comes, with his face to foe and a smile on his face as though all was well. We checked the enemy then and whipped them the next day handsomely. Took many prisoners. All we regretted was that our companions were not there to share our victories. It must be hard for a mother to lose such a son as Philo, but such is the fortune of war. May he enjoy all the blessings of the next life. He deserves it if any one does. I do not know how I can send this but will try. I knew Ellis for the last few years at Minneiska, Minn.

> *Yours respectfully and sincerely,*
> *S. O. Seymour*

(A copy of this letter may be found in Miller, *Ellis Family* 57-58.)

Having barely gotten over the shock of the death of John Ellis—husband of Susan and father of the ten Ellis children—the entire family now had to deal with the death of Susan's son, Cobe. As recently as June, Susan had written to Cobe, encouraging him to "be of good cheer as you can in your situation and perform every known duty to your God and your Country." Susan Ellis had selected Cobe to be her support in her declining years, and now she had lost the promise of the help of this special son.

The death of Cobe must have cast a cloud over Samuel and Silence and their new family as well. How would Silence bear the loss of her brother, and take on the extra care that she would have provided to her grieving mother? Their oldest son, Myron, had been born in 1859 and now, in the midst of the grief, Milo H. Miller was born on September 4, 1863. One can only hope that the new arrival and his older brother would have brought some relief and happiness to Susan Ellis and to Samuel and Silence.

With the death of Cobe, Samuel K. Miller had lost a brother-in-law, with whom he had spent some time several years before the outbreak of the war. When he volunteered in 1864, Samuel's four Ellis cousins were already in the service.

The story of the Ellis family and the family of Samuel and Silence, however unique in its details, was being played out in all parts of America. In both the North and South, men were entering the Civil War and leaving behind families, some of them quite large and some already having suffered deep losses. As the Civil War raged on, this was a continuing topic of concern to townsfolk everywhere.

Chapter 4

Why Did He Volunteer?

Why would a man with a good trade, a wife and two small children leave them behind to go into the Union Army? The historical context of the times and Samuel's own personal belief system most likely contributed to Samuel's decision.

One month after the fall of Fort Sumter, Congress passed a law enabling the Federal government to pay a bounty—a payment—of up to $300 for those willing to volunteer for service. The Confederacy provided for a bounty of $50 after three or more years of service, which was later revised upward to $100. (Perri 424-453)

The bounty scheme was adjusted during the war to allow state and local areas to contribute to the bounty pool. Provision was also made for widows to have a portion of the bounty upon the death of their husbands. Eventually the total bounty funds available in some locations increased significantly. In one county in New York State, the bounty reached $1,000. The funds to make the payments were provided by taxation, bond issues and donations. These bounties enabled families at home to survive and added to the ability of returning soldiers to return to civilian life with some resources to restart their lives. (Ibid)

The Enrollment Act of 1863 was passed in March of that year, specifying that all able-bodied men between twenty and forty-five years of age would be drafted. To ensure that the Union Army's need for large numbers of soldiers was actually met, quotas were assigned to each state, which would in turn allocate the quota to districts. The law also specified that all districts would be notified of their quotas, and the districts were urged to fill their quotas before the established deadline.

However, the law excused people from military service if they were able to pay a fee of three hundred dollars. Further, it was possible for men to get a substitute to serve in their place. With the volunteers and substitutions, the end result was that only a small percentage of all who served were drafted. These practices led to the accusation that this was a rich man's war and a poor man's fight. By World War I, the bounty system was no longer implemented because there were so many abuses. (Ibid)

Since Samuel met the qualification of being under the forty-five age limit, he entered the military as part of the Turnersville quota, and was paid $500 as his bounty. Might he have been drafted if he had not volunteered? Possibly, but it is apparent that he had other motivations to join the army. Milo H. Miller stated some years later that his father, Samuel, had told him, "There needed to be a Miller in this fight to save the Union."

Samuel's letters reveal several aspects of his reasons for entering the service, as well as some of his closely-held tenets and beliefs.

This first message was sent only a few days after he left home:

> *September 6, 1864   Camp Reynolds* [Pennsylvania]   #1

> *I am in good spirits and not sorry that I have volunteered for my country. I am well, and have many merry times. Last night I heard praying and swearing, dancing and fiddling and singing. As for my part, I did neither. I bought myself a Testament to instruct myself when a soldier boy.*

Several days later, he told about being challenged about why he was going:

> *September 12, 1864   Camp Reynolds* [Pennsylvania]   #2

> *I saw Hiram when at Nelson's station. Said he—Do you not hate to go? No—said I—am going to fight for my country. I have not written to him yet.*

It is difficult to determine the role that money played in his decision to volunteer, but the support that those funds provided were always at the top of his mind:

> *September 17, 1864   Camp Reynolds [Pennsylvania]   #3*
> *[finished in Washington, D.C.]*
> *We got our government bounty pay, that is, $133.33. I will send you in this letter ten dollars, and the next letter I write I will send ten dollars more and so on until I get it all home. I bought me a pair of boots, which cost me nine dollars in Baltimore, and sold my shoes for $1.50, so my boots stands me $7.50. Silence, get the boys or some lady to get you winter wood. The weather is beautiful indeed, the roads are dusty, the sun very warm and pleasant. We have nice quarters and good grub, that is, coffee and bread and pork. Send me when the opportunity the* Morning Star *[newspaper].*

Apparently the bounty of $500 was intended to be paid in increments, not all at once.

The people back in Hartstown had sharply different opinions about his volunteering for the Army:

> *September 26, 1864   Camp of the 211th Pa. Volunteers   #4*
>
> *Hiram told me that Mayo thought I done right, but Eliza thought it awful. Let me know about the draft, who was drafted.*

As the weeks dragged on, it's clear that Silence was getting a lot of grief from the neighbors about Samuel having left his family to volunteer in the Army. His response to her letters shows his strong reactions to her concerns:

> *October 11, 1864   Bermuda Hundred   #7*
>
> *You said in your letter that the folks blamed you for letting me come to war. Just tell them if they say anything to you again for me that I wished them to attend to their own business and let you alone while I am here in the service of my country. Tell them to wait until I come*

home and I will talk to them myself, and just say to Mag for me to keep her mouth shut and keep her guts warm. Tell them not to blame you for anything that I have done. Do not concern yourself about me. I am well and hearty, more so than I have [been] for six months.

Several month later, his letters became more pointed about why he left his family to serve in the army:

January 8, 1865   Headquarters Army of the Potomac   #22

Silence, what does the people think, about the coming draft. Are they making any preparation for it, or do they intend all to skiddadl for Canada, or hire Rebel substitutes as they did before. I think I done or took a wise plan for coming in when I did, for it certainly would have caught me this time if I had not been drafted before. On the other hand, if I had not come I should have been kept poor by paying out money all the time trying to raise volunteers, so I think I am making money by coming and, if the Lord spares my life, I can enjoy it when I get home, and that in such a way that it will please God and man.

What does George McGranahan think about the war now—also about the draft? I can tell you the reason you did not get more wood cut—because you are an abolitionist wife. What do they think now about my going to the Army? I would like to talk to some of them Copperheads. I think I could tell them some things that would not set very well on their stomachs.

When Samuel learned that Silence was getting a lot of grief from some of the neighbors because he had joined the Union Army, he viewed his neighbors' actions as vengeful. He was sensitive to how his decision was being interpreted by the townspeople of Hartstown. He was both furious at them and protective of Silence. Samuel had volunteered because he believed that the Union must be preserved. He also was focused on providing for his family, and he reviewed his decision proudly to join the Union Army, thereby earning a bounty that would support them while he was away. In any case, Samuel's principles did not allow him to look kindly on the antiwar stance of the "Copperheads," and he disparaged those who were not fulfilling their responsibilities to their country.

It is also possible that some of his neighbors viewed both Samuel and Silence as abolitionists because they attended the Free Will Baptist Church, which took a leading role in the United States in ardently opposing slavery on moral and religious grounds.

In any case, Samuel had also volunteered in order to serve his country, and he turned to the Bible for guidance on how to fulfill his duty as a soldier. From these brief excerpts and all his correspondence during his nine months of service, it is clear that Samuel's sense of purpose never wavered.

Chapter 5

From Meadville to Bermuda Hundred:
His Comrades

Samuel had journeyed from his boyhood home in Ohio as far north as St. Paul, Minnesota and throughout the east as a drover. He had experienced some of the rough and tumble of people during those travels. When he entered the service in Meadville, he encountered a wide variety of men; some he admired, and others he did not.

September 8, 1864   Camp Reynolds, Pennsylvania   #1

We left Meadville on Monday at 10 A.M. for Ravenna, Ohio. There we changed cars for Wellsville and Pittsburgh, thence to our present location. Our captain has not come yet but expect him today. There are about 5,000 boys here with their blues on. There are about 800 tents up. The soldier boys are most all married men, some 50 to 55 years old. But the majority are middle-aged men that have done as I have done—left their homes, some with wives only and the rest with wives and from one to four or five little ones that are dear to them as mine is to me.

September 12, 1864   Camp Reynolds   #2

We have the best-hearted lot of men in our company that I ever saw. So clever and sociable—and a great many professors. No swearing and cursing like there is in most of the companies. I have heard more wickedness since I came to camp than I ever heard in all my life and travels.

It must have been comforting to both Samuel and Silence that he was in the company of men from Crawford County and vicinity whom he had known before he volunteered, and his letters reflect the companionship and support they provided one another.

October 31, 1864   *Camp Bermuda Hundred,*   *#11*
                            Butler Headquarters

I believe I never told you who all belonged to Company A that I was acquainted with—Isaac Graff, Osker Lee from the Lake, Jerry Millen Heandy from where Greenawalt lives. I. P. Kean from Shermans Corners and Preacher Rogers that used to preach at Adamsville. Old drunken Bill Brown's oldest boy is in Company A. Mr. Rogers and a man by the name of Thurston were chosen or detailed when we first came here to guard an ammunition train, so you perceive he is not with us—but was up this morning to get his news and he gave me a Morning Star. I tell you I gave it a good perusal. It done me more good [than] *if I had eaten my dinner.*

We also have an excellent chaplain in our regiment from Venango County near Franklin, that preached yesterday at the Company headquarters outdoors. A very large audience were out in attendance.

Throughout his nine months of service, Samuel maintained contact with his friends in the 211th and with relatives stationed near him.

Chapter 6

Picket Duty—Getting to Know You: Picket Duty, a Surprise Attack

Soon after arriving at the Bermuda Hundred, Samuel began to experience the war first-hand. He was put onto picket duty in front of the Union lines, and was located very close to the Confederate picket lines, perhaps only twenty yards apart. Here is his description of the duties of the picket:

October 23, 1864   *Bermuda Hundred, Virginia*   *#9*

This evening we go out on picket duty and remain there 24 hours, then we are relieved by others. It requires 600 men to guard the line which is perhaps 3 miles in length. It is easy duty. We stand 2 hours on and 2 hours off, and day time 1 hour on and 4 off, etc. So goes the duties of war.

The pickets were to observe the enemy as an early warning system. When the pickets spotted movements of the enemy's troops, they would convey this valuable information to their regimental command, who would then issue orders to counteract the enemy's maneuvers.

Often, however, due to their close proximity to each other, the pickets from each side interacted with one another. This was the case with Samuel and his fellow pickets. Picket duty gave him a very close view of his adversaries, not just the short distance between the opposing picket lines, but in face-to-face conversations and trading of goods and newspapers. In fact, he got to know the enemy soldiers very well. His comments about the connections between enemy pickets is almost casual, but these are really quite remarkable exchanges.

Samuel served on picket duty from early October until mid December,
and these were his some of his observations and experiences:

October 3, 1864   *Bermuda Hundred*   *#5*

We are now in front of the Rebels, about on line between the two places
which our armies [are] *contending for—that* [is] *Petersburg and*
Richmond. Our army is fighting on our right and left, which we can
hear very distinctly from where we lay. We are laying in the strongest
fortifications, the old soldiers say, that is, except Grant's, where his
army lays or is fortified. The Rebels have a fortification right on our
front, probably 3/4 of a mile. Our picket lines lay between these two
fortifications where we and the Rebels have to stand picket.

The first night I was out, there was 6 Rebels came to our lines.
Oh, but they were glad when they got to us! They said there was
twenty-seven in one company that said wanted to come to our lines.
The weather here was warm and pleasant until a day or two [ago].
It has rained some this morning. About daylight we were routed out
of our tents in a hurry to the Breast Works [trenches or chest-high
structures intended to help protect the soldiers from enemy fire]. *The*
alarm was that the Rebels was going to make a charge, but they
failed to come. Our Batbies [batteries] *gave them about fifty shots*
but they never returned the compliment. So we went back to camp
probably 50 yards. I expect tonight I will be on picket. We have a
great many that is considerable cowards. I am going to do my duty.
I think the thing is coming to a close as fast as can be done. We
could see them fight over on Malvern Hill across the James River, a
distance of 5 or 6 miles. We could see the dust and smoke and shells
bursting in the air.

October 9, 1864   *Bermuda Hundred,*
                          Camp Near Point of Rocks   *#11*
                          [Letter to his brother-in-law Enoch Ellis]

Our boys are now within four miles of Richmond. The [word] *came*
in yesterday that the Rebs were evacuating Richmond and were going
to Danville to concentrate there, but there are so many reports come

every day that you cannot tell what is truth or what is not. The first night we stood picket we took in 7 Rebs into our lines. There were 5 that came in on my post. I tell you they were glad when they got into our lines. They were poorly clad and it rained all night and cold. They were very near froze.

October 11, 1864   Bermuda Hundred, Near Point of Rocks   #7

The war is about played out. The Johnnies are coming into our lines every day. The Georgians have thrown out their arms and declare they will not fight any more. Grant has given them the permission of crossing our lines if the Rebels refuse them crossing their own lines. We have to stand picket about every other night. We can see the Rebs and talk to them and exchange newspapers with them—also trade coffee for their tobacco. They are awful afraid of us. They tell us when they are ordered to fire upon us they say they will shoot over our heads and they want us to do the same. They say if Lincoln is reelected that they are all gone up.

Like many other Union soldiers, Samuel was too optimistic about the ending of the war. He did not realize it then, but the war in Virginia would last another six months:

November 14, 1864   Bermuda Hundred   #13

The poor Reb soldiers in our front, that we can see every day, say they get one pint of flour or meal a day for their rations, and a piece of fresh beef one half inches square, that is, they say so, them that come into our lines.

Last week there were 24 come to our lines Saturday night. One came across yesterday in broad daylight. One came over to us. He said that most all that was in the fortifications would come over but they dare not only as they can watch their opportunity and then they have to watch until them that [are] opposed to deserting get asleep, and then they are off for our lines in a hurry. I will give you an idea of our picket line on a piece of paper so you can see the position we are placed in, etc.

November 23, 1964   Camp Bermuda Hundred   #14

I am . . .very well today. I took a bad cold laying on the ground at nights on picket. It settled in my back, and has given me a diarrhea, but the doctor has given me some powder to take. He also excused me from duty. Otherwise feel very well.

After a period of relative calm along the picket lines, the Confederates launched a surprise attack which caught the Union forces unaware:

November 26, 1864   Bermuda Hundred   #15

On last night a week ago the Jonnies made a break upon our picket line about half past 8 o'clock in the evening, with a strong force of two brigades which was about five or six thousand, so says their own newspapers. They come slipping upon us, the night being very dark and our line of works or picket line running the whole length through the timber, or woods, made it rather dark, or just before the moon rose. Well, they came within ten rods of us before they opened fire, which they done rather briskly.

Nearly half of our boys had laid down to sleep and some had gone to sleep. I had set down by a little fire we had—off it went, bang-bang-bang it went all along the line. We all was ready in an instant, for we was expecting some move for several days that they had made their brags they were going to gobble our picket line. We, of course, thought they would give us some signs of it, but at all events, the thing is over and God spared my life. I thank Him for it.

The Rebs took our line with fifty-three prisoners from us, that is out of our regiment. They took our lines for eight miles. They took, in all, about 600 prisoners. There was one killed in our regiment, 3 wounded etc. There was 5 men in our post, there are 5 men in every post, and the posts are about as far apart as from the front of our house to the upper end of our garden. We all sprang to our rifle pits and commenced the combat, but their number being so much greater that ours, we were obliged to retreat but not until we gave them six or seven rounds. A great many of our boys left their rifle pits altogether. I tell you the Balls [minie balls] *flew thick for about two hours. We stood to our post until the Rebs made a charge. I saw them first—then they was within 1 1/2 rods of us. The word was fire—so we did. We gave them five well aimed shots, then ran for the woods. The balls came whistling some then, but we all escaped unhurt. So it went.*

In late November, Samuel's regiment marched many miles to a new encampment where they were in sight of Petersburg. This move seems to be the end of his involvement in picket duty:

December 1, 1864   Army of the Potomac Front of Petersburgh   #16

Since I wrote you last we have done some marching. We got marching orders on last Saturday evening with 4 days rations. On Sunday about 10 o'clock we packed up our things and started but not knowing where we was or what place was destined for us—but at alevance [?] we marched 7 miles then encamped for the night. Next morning we started at daylight and marched all day reaching place of destination which being in all the distance of 21 miles. We only stayed for two nights then we got orders again to march with four days rations, taking back tracks for some point, but did not know where until we reached this place. We can see Petersburgh very easily from where we are encamped. I don't think we will stay here long, for General Meade does not want raw troops here. Therefore, I think we shant be here a great while. I hope to goodness they will take us from here, for there is not a more dangerous place on the whole front.

Here is Samuel's response to his wife's question about where he slept when he was not on picket duty:

December 5, 1864   Headquarters Army of the Potomac   #17

You wanted to know how we slept. When our two hours were off picket, we take our rubber blankets and spread them on the ground. We generally wear our overcoats then we lay down and snooze by the fire. Down where we came from we had to go on picket every other night, but where we are now we do not have anything of that kind to do.

The pickets where we are now fire at each other day and night. Their rifles are telescope seven shooters [capable of shooting seven bullets without reloading], *and all the way* [the only way] *they can get to their posts is through ditches dug in the ground 6 feet deep so the Rebs cannot see them going to and coming. We are drilled 3 hours every day. That is all the work we have to do until further ordered.*

The surprise attack on the Union lines resulted in a far less cordial relationship between the competing picket lines!

December 18, 1864   Army of the Potomac, Virginia   #19

The war is still going on. The Rebs are deserting daily by hundreds. General Butler has taken the railroad from the Rebs where we first lay at Dutch Canal, which is the last road they had between Richmond and Petersburgh. I do not see how they can stand it much longer. The impression of all [is] *that the Rebs cannot contend longer than spring. I hope it may be so, for we are all tired of soldiers life, although I am not discouraged nor homesick or nothing of that kind. But it just seems to me as though we all should be home by summer, but I shall be contented with my lot—let it be what it may.*

From Samuel's letters, one sees a pattern of Confederate soldiers who were ill-fed and ill-clothed. Those conditions drove many of them to desert, despite significant risks in doing so. That the Confederates were able to fight so vigorously for so long is remarkable, given their lack of adequate food and clothing. Samuel seems to show no strong animosity nor hatred to the enemy he faced, though it was also clear that he was dedicated to being a good, loyal soldier.

Chapter 7

Samuel's Experience in
Battles and Skirmishes

In addition to the combat experiences described in Samuel's letters relating to his picket duty, he was to experience several other encounters, skirmishes, and battles.

While still at Bermuda Hundred, he observed shots being fired on Confederate fortifications:

> *October 23, 1864   Bermuda Hundred   #9*
>
> *Our batteries with 40 guns opened and fired 100 shots into the Rebel's fortification perhaps a mile distant, killing five men in one tent and how many more we did not learn, so said a Rebel deserter which came into our lines that night, but the Rebels never replied one shot. They were, I presume, afraid.*

From what I would surmise about the courage of the Confederates, I rather doubt that they were afraid, but at least that is what Samuel assumed that day.

At times, it seems that Samuel was fortunate to be given assignments that kept him some distance from the action. Here is an example:

> *October 31, 1864   Camp Bermuda Hundred, Butler Headquarters #11*
>
> *I wrote to you once before that myself and I.P. Kean were detailed to cut lumber for hospitals, which will probably take us 3 weeks. There*

are about 200 men to work, which keeps us from the battlefield, if there should be any battles. Our colonel talks some of us taking to Washington to guard forts. There are nearly a fourth of our regiment sick with the ague [a chill or fit of shivering]. *I hope he will succeed in accomplishing it. We are not well enough drilled for this place. We can see the bomb shells fly at night and burst as plain as the fingers on your hand, but are not nearer than one and a half miles from camp.*

Tell Ab and Nate the canal is finished, all but the blowing out the ends. The Rebs throw shells into the canal every day and every night, but our men have bomb proofs made so they can run into when shot at. We expect a big battle in a few days. Last Thursday and Thursday night there was an awful battle near Petersburg. We could hear the cannonading just as plain as though they were not more than one mile off—but was some three miles distant. The skies were as light—I was going to say, as day. We have not yet heard the result of the battle.

One experience is almost humorous, and shows how close he came to being captured or being killed:

December 5, 1864   Headquarters Army of the Potomac   #17

I received a letter from Enoch yesterday morning, making inquiry whether I was taken prisoner. He had heard so. I did come very near being taken. The Rebs came so close to me that they halted me and four others that we had to give leg bail [run] *for our safety. The Rebs threw some 10 or 15 balls after us but fortunately did not take effect, but they came very close to our heads.*

It is hard to imagine Samuel and his mates choosing to run for their lives, with the Confederates shooting at them as they ran. That special effort took rather amazing leadership by someone to choose to take that risk rather than staying and being captured or killed, and to lead the other men in taking that risk. It also was a gallant effort by the men involved to run as fast as they could, with bullets whizzing by their heads while they ran for their lives. That was quite likely the closest Samuel came to losing his life.

Samuel was involved in a very important expedition, known as the Weldon Expedition which took place from December 7 through December 11, 1864. Many miles of railroad track were destroyed, rendering the Weldon Railroad, which transported supplies to the Rebel forces in Petersburg, inoperative. Noah Andre Trudeau, in his book *The Last Citadel: Petersburg, Virginia June 1864-April 1865,* discusses this expedition and its outcome:

> *Writing on December 14, Warren estimated that his men had marched about 100 miles in six days and destroyed about seventeen miles of track between the Nottaway and Meherrin rivers . . . ."* (Trudeau 284-285)

> In his report, General Meade, noting General Warren's report, stated that *"the result of the expedition was the complete destruction of sixteen miles of the railroad, preventing its use beyond Hicksford, which unless the damages are repaired, is in effect depriving the enemy its use beyond Weldon."* (Ibid)

> Robert E. Lee stated that *"they destroyed about six miles of railroad, so the superintendent reports, & burned some small bridges . . . . (*Ibid)

Trudeau summarizes:

> *Warren's six-day operation (variously referred to as the Weldon, the Belfield, the Hicksford, or the Applejack Raid) dealt Lee's already brittle supply chain a serious though not fatal blow. It exacerbated a difficult food situation and contributed greatly to the hardships that Lee's army would face in the coming months . . . . Somehow or other the Confederate government and the railroad managed to find the necessary men and materials to re-build the sixteen miles General Warren had destroyed. Early in March 1865 the road was opened all the way from Weldon to Stoney Creek, but it was in operation only for a brief period before events at Petersburg led to the abandonment of the whole line.* (Ibid.)

Clearly, then, this was a very significant expedition in its role of cutting off supplies for the Confederate Army. This is how Samuel K. Miller viewed that action:

December 14, 1864   Army of the Potomac, Petersburgh, Virginia   #18

The last time I wrote you we had marching orders. On Friday evening about dark we all pulled up stakes, as we called it, and started, but not knowing where, but at ever [any] rate, we marched about 2 miles and encamped for the night. And just about the time we barely got at pitching our tents for the night, it began to rain and snow and kept it up until morning daylight, when it ceased. We lay there all day.

Now I will give you a full detail of our road we made, or were to have made. On Saturday evening about dark we pulled up and started for Rebeldom. There were 6 regiments of us together. We marched 22 miles through the mud until 4 o'clock in the morning, where we halted for the night, where we encamped amongst the Rebs. But before we got started in the morning again the order was to counter march, that is, to come back. The reason we were sent there was to stand as reserve to build fortifications and hold them while the calebry [cavalry] of one thousand and two corps of old infantry were driving the enemy and capturing horses, cattle, sheep, hogs, turkeys, chickens, carts, buggies, sulkeys. Everything they could carry away with them. Some had looking glasses, chairs, trunks, dishes, everything you can mention. They also burnt every house, barn, out building. They came to one place—they got 30 barrels of apple whiskey, which they drank and destroyed and tore up 30 miles of the South Side railroad, which was their only road they had of importance for transporting provisions.

We took 400 prisoners, 2100 Negroes, including women and children. I saw a great many of them myself. I tell you they were tickled to get into the Union Army. Our army that went out on the road was one hundred thousand strong. The raid was made across the Black River near the line between Virginia and North Carolina on what is called the South Side Railroad. You can find where it is location by looking and the map (X) [map not available]. When we started back with our brigade at 3 o'clock Sunday afternoon, the army train had about half of them passed, that is, infantry, artillery, wagons train, ambulances, cattle, etc.

The first house we came past on our road back was about half mile on this side—where we [camped] over Sunday—[it] was a beautiful house which was lit on fire and burning nicely. When we came by, all the out buildings and Negro quarters were also set fire and burned and the whites had all left, but a few blacks. Then we came along a short distance farther where [there] was a beautiful house—as good a house as Robert McMichael's house—was burned. I saw that burn. The next we come to was a meeting house that was burned. To make the story short, we burnt every house and building along the road for twenty-two miles and killed everything in the shape of horses, cattle, sheep, hogs, turkeys and chickens, and brought everything with us that we could carry. We got back to our quarters about 3 o'clock Monday morning. When we came back our quarters were occupied by another regiment, then we marched two miles and encamped in the woods for two days and a night.

Since 3 o'clock on Sunday the weather has been excessive cold, almost as cold as last New Year's Day. We very near came perishing to death laying on the ground. I presume we would have frozen if we had not kept on log fire all night.

So it goes in the army. Although I am content and have stood the march better or as well as any of them. Our knapsack and haversack with four days rations and harness and guns weight in the neighborhood of 80 pounds, which we carried 44 miles in twenty-four hours. We have the praise of General Hancock, the best regiment for traveling in the Division, or corps. So that closed our campaign raid. Night before last there were three companies of Rebs came across to our lines, so you see that is reducing the Rebellion at a fast rate.

Toward the end of January, Samuel observed from a distance an exchange of gunfire:

January 24, 1865   Headquarters Army of the Potomac   #24

This Wednesday morning about 4 o'clock I got tired sleeping and laying so I thought that I would spend an hour or so in writing to one that I love dearly. While I am writing the gun boats are throwing their deadly shots at each other down on the James River. Night before last the Rebs made an attack upon us down on the James at the Dutch Canal where we lay last fall, but the Rebs were badly whipped. We sunk two rams [Confederate ships reinforced with iron bows in order to pierce the wooden hulls of Union ships, thereby rendering them inoperative] *for them and blew up one and disabled two. The Rebs have made the second attack and what the result will be this time we know not.*

Several weeks later, viewing a large battle, Samuel thought the end was near:

February 9, 1865   Headquarters 9th Army Corps   #27

This is Thursday morning about one o'clock. I am upon Guard the after part of the night and a beautiful morning it is. The moon shines bright as day

There has been a great battle in progress upon our left. The Rebs made a move in that direction with the intention of breaking our lines, but was severely whipped by the fifth Corps which took the South Side railroad, but were repulsed, but our boys rallying again and retook the Road and are holding and fortifying it. I have not heard our loss or the Rebs, but I will let you know in my next letter. My regiment is out, but was not engaged in the battle. There were 70,000 men there but only one corps engaged, which is about 30,000. The Rebs said to our boys when they got there—Yanks, you will get what you come for—but I think it was the reverse. They got what they didn't want, a good whipping. The intention of Grant is to take the Danville Road, then the Rebs will have to evacuate Petersburgh. Them were the only two roads they had to get their supplies on for their army. I think if they get several good thrashings they will come to terms of peace . . . . This fight about which I have spoken was about 12 miles to our left, or in other words, due South.

As promised, in his next letter he told Silence more about that battle:

February 11, 1865   Headquarters 9th Army Corps   #28

I also stated in my last letter that there was a great battle upon our left. Our regiment was called out but was not in the fight. The 5th and 6th Corps done all the fighting, and whipped the Jonnies very bad.

We advanced our line two miles and lengthened it six miles and built breastworks sufficiently strong enough to hold them at bay. The Rebs charged the 5th and 6th three times but were repulsed each time with a heavy loss. Our loss in killed was about 200 and wounded was about double the number of killed. Lyman Kilgrove was in the battle, I think. He either belongs to 5th or the 6th Corps, I cannot say which. Also, Jim Davidson, William Trimble, William McMaster, William McQuiston, Robert Bowden, Wallace Brown, but I think they all escaped unhurt, or at least I did not see any of their names on the list of wounded. The Rebs seemed to be down on peace nowadays. They cry—fight it out—or independence to the last. I think Grant will give them all they want by the time the roads get settled in the spring, if not before.

Even in the darkest moments of war, there are some spectacular, but tragic sights. Samuel and the rest of his Mounted Pioneer comrades were kept far enough away from the battles to be safe able to respond quickly to the Ninth Corps needs for engineering and supply emergencies and needs. They had somewhat of a "grandstand seat" to watch some of the sights and sounds. Toward the end of the war, he observed what would have been almost a fireworks display, if it had not been so death-dealing.

March 30, 1865   Headquarters Ninth Corp   #35

Last night at about half past 10 o'clock, the Rebels massed troops in front of Petersburgh, but was unsuccessful in making the attack. They were received with a warm reception from our batteries, which opened out on them. I never saw such cannon. You would have thought all the stars in the Heavens were falling. The night was dark and every shell that was thrown looked like a star shooting until it burst, which would make a large flash of light.

Chapter 8

The Horrors of War:
Hangings and Surgeries

Samuel was deeply affected during his time in the Civil War by the horrible sights one encounters in war. In December 1864, he witnessed a hanging of two deserters from the Union Army. It was done in a way that conveyed a vivid message to a large group of soldiers that desertions would be dealt with in an ignominious manner. Not only would the deserters be hung, but they would be further humiliated by being hung in front of a large number of their comrades. Samuel was shocked by what he saw, and captured the feelings that would have been shared by 13,000 men that day:

December 14, 1864   *Army of the Potomac, Petersburgh*   *#18*

In the meantime there were two men executed for desertion from our army to the Rebs. They were out of the 137th New York Volunteers. They deserted last July and [were] captured a short time ago. It was the hardest scene I ever beheld in all my travels. They were the boldest fellows I ever saw. One of them smoked a cigar upon the scaffold. The death warrant was read and then a prayer, then their faces were covered with white cloths, their hands and feet tied together and marched a couple paces to the front, and then the ropes adjusted about their necks, then the spring of the trap door was touched, which dropped quicker than flash. There they hung between Heaven and Earth. What a sight to see souls sent to Eternity! They never made any confession nor did they care where their souls went, for they were very wicked men. So that finishes that subject, with adding that there were about 13,000 present to witness the scene.

Beyond the horror of what he saw, Samuel reflected on the religious aspect of what he experienced. He mentioned the *soul* of those men, and where those souls were headed.

Several months later, he would again encounter one of the horrible sights of war, the results of amputations following battle. By this time, Samuel had been transferred into the Mounted Pioneer Corp, a group of twenty-five men drawn from several regiments and attached to the Union 9th Army Corp. This scene starts with his description of the battle of Fort Stedman in March 1865:

March 27, 1865   *Headquarters 9th Army Corps*   *#34*

I must also let you know of the great battle fought Saturday morning. [This was the battle of Fort Stedman]. *It commenced half past four o'clock and lasted until 8—fought 3 ½* [hours]. *The Rebs massed there troops the night before unbeknown to us. Their forces numbering about thirty thousand and came through our picket line and cut our abaties* [abatis: singular or plural, an arrangement of tree trunks and branches placed to impede a charging army] *in front of our Breastworks and forts and entered Fort Stedman and took all prisoners that were in the fort. Then into the camp and took a great many prisoners before they were awake. Then the Ball opened! By that time the Rebs had captured two of our forts and turned the cannon and commenced shelling us. Those that were engaged in it said they never saw harder fighting. It was hard telling which would come out victorious but at last the Rebs began to waver and in the meantime all the new regiments that have laid all winter in reserve, which will number 6 thousand, made a charge upon the Rebs, which made them skiddadle. We retook our forts and twenty-seven hundred prisoners and killed about three thousand, that is, killed and wounded.*

I heard the fight. You could scarcely hear yourself talk for so much firing—both cannon and musketry. The battle was only 1 ½ miles from where we lay. Our regiment was in the fight. Their loss was slight. One man in my company was wounded in the hand. The Rebs calculated to break our lines and destroy our railroad and take City Point, but they failed in doing it. I saw all the prisoners. They were the hardest looking men I ever saw. There were dirty, ragged and a great many without shoes. Oh, such men I never—they are far dirtier looking than the railroad puddies [a dark pudding served to passengers riding in railway trains].

Samuel was fortunate to be some distance from the battle, but soon thereafter he came upon the aftermath of the battle while the wounded were being treated:

It took our troops and the Rebs all day to bury their dead. A great many fell into our hands. Also a great many wounded, which we had to take care of. I saw four flour barrels full of legs and arms taken off by our doctors. Our loss was 5 hundred killed and wounded. It was an awful sight to see those limbs. They were most all Rebel legs and arms. There was a fight on our extreme left the same day. We captured two lines of works [fortified structures of any kind designed to strengthen a position in battle] *and took nine hundred prisoners.*

General Sheridan and his entire cavalry force is encamped in the woods in our rear, perhaps one fourth of a mile. Such blowing of bugles you never heard. It makes me feel heart sick. He intends going to form a junction with Sherman. Then you will hear of the greatest battles fought yet, or they will surrender. Charley Carothers thinks it cannot last longer than the middle of May.

Samuel's descriptions of what he observed after the battle, the containers of amputated arms and legs still in the open and the sound of the bugle that caused such sadness in him, are evidence of the profound effect the war was having on him. These deeply troubling experiences would undoubtedly remain in his memory for the rest of his life.

In his letters, Samuel talked of "taking care of his soul." Certainly in 1865, there was little or no reference to what happened to one's soul as a result of being in a war and seeing the horrors of war first-hand. Samuel may not have suffered physical wounds, but was his *soul* wounded?

Only in recent years has there been attention focused on what happens to one's soul in combat. Edward Tick has addressed this issue in his book, *War and the Soul: Healing Our Nation's Veterans from Post-Traumatic Stress Disorder.*

. . . PTSD (post-traumatic stress syndrome) is primarily a moral, spiritual, and aesthetic disorder—in effect, not a psychological but a soul disorder. All of its aspects concern dimensions of the soul, inasmuch as the soul is the part of us that responds to morality, spirituality, aesthetics aimed at them directly in this context. (Tick 108)

Having observed at close range the hangings and the amputations following battle, Samuel would have had those images implanted on his soul forever. Perhaps because he was forty-two years old and was more mature than many of his younger comrades, he was able to realize that those experiences were having a deep impact on his whole being, and on his soul.

My father, James M. Miller, served as a forward artillery observer in World War I. His unit, the 314th Field Artillery, served in France and played a critical role in the Battle of the Argonne Forest. After four weeks in that battle, Dad was incapacitated and taken to a hospital in Orleans, France, then later to a hospital in Lakewood, New Jersey to recover. In his letters, he talks of trying to get rid of the nightmares, dreams that never left him. His soul, too, was wounded by his experiences in that war. His experiences in World War I, and his means of coping with the effects on his soul, can be the topic of another book!

Chapter 9

Living Conditions:
Food, Clothing and Shelter

Because Silence wanted to know about his location, his shelter, his food and his clothing, Samuel was very forthcoming and descriptive about these matters. From this correspondence, we gain very detailed descriptions of Samuel's living conditions. Often Samuel would request that Silence send him supplies. The logistics of getting letters, food and clothing from northwestern Pennsylvania to the front lines near Petersburg, and back, are rather amazing; that letters and goods flowed so rapidly and effectively is somewhat of a marvel.

He was asked by Silence to describe his living conditions, and his responses paint an interesting picture of his shelter (or lack thereof) and his experiences in acquiring food, clothing and shelter during his nine months of service.

In the very early days of his service, while in or near Washington, D.C., he answered her questions.

> *September 17, 1864*   *Camp Reynolds, Pennsylvania*   *#3*
> [mailed from Washington, D.C.]

> *It* [his partial bounty payment] *bought me a pair of boots, which cost me nine dollars in Baltimore, and sold my shoes for $1.50, so my boots cost me $7.50. Silence, get the boys or some lady to get you winter wool . . . . We have nice quarters and good grub—that is, coffee and bread and pork. Send me when the opportunity the Morning Star* [newspaper].

Many of Samuel's letters raise interesting questions, which lead to our speculation, and perhaps to further research. For example, boots were a valuable item during the Civil War. The soldiers were issued one pair, which would have worn out rather quickly with all their marching. Where would they find a replacement pair? Who would have a ready supply? Did he buy the boots from a sutler, a person who went to the field to sell items for which the soldiers would have a great need? If the person who sold Samuel a pair of boots took a pair of Samuel's shoes as a partial payment, to whom would that person sell the used shoes?

It is not surprising that Samuel would have written home for some of his clothing and supplies. Lower-ranking soldiers were issued uniforms, but officers had to buy their own uniforms. Many companies made uniforms for their soldiers, some made on foot-powered treadle sewing machines. Those were possibly Singer sewing machines, since that company had been in business since 1851 and had invented the treadle in the 1850s. Some of the garments were hand-sewn, and even the machine-made garments were finished by hand.

The soldiers were not supplied very generously. A typical soldier would receive some items only once a year; drawers (undergarments), shirts, and a pair of socks. One can only imagine how those items fared after a few weeks or months, even with their best efforts to clean those garments. The soldiers were issued wool trousers, which must have been rather uncomfortable in Southern summers! They wore ankle-high shoes, known as "brogans," and often brought a vest from home, since that was not issued. Another item was a sack coat, which was used for field duty. It was easy to make and cheap. Those who wore glasses usually brought them from home.

Apart from the uniform itself, they received a knapsack which contained half of a tent and a rubber-coated canvas blanket they could put on the ground or when it rained. A blanket was strapped to the top of the knapsack. In addition, they received a fry pan, spatula and canteen. Finally, they were issued a haversack for carrying food, a catridge box, a musket, cap box and bayonet. (Information from *A Union Soldier's Uniform from the Civil War, around 1865.*)

During the Petersburg campaign, the weather varied widely, from very high temperatures in the summer to snow, ice and cold in the winter, and the items issued to the soldiers either did not last long enough or did not serve the soldiers' needs during the various seasons. Fortunately, the postal system was able to deliver reliably what Silence sent to him at his request. Clearly, Samuel was not alone in receiving some of his clothing and food from Silence in Hartstown.

Samuel and his regiment arrived in Virginia in late September, and he described his "lodging" to Silence:

September 26, 1864 Camp of the 211ᵗʰ Pennsylvania Volunteers #4

I wrote you last at Washington and now we are camped in Virginia, about two miles in the rear of Bermuda Hundred, or in other words, two miles from the James River, where Butler made the Rebels skiddadel last May. Butler's whole force lays in sight of our camp. We all saw the old general last Saturday passing by. He is a good-looking man and a brave man, I think from his appearance.

We left Camp Reynolds last Saturday a week ago, and arrived this place Thursday evening dusk. We lay on the ground the first night. Next day we all went to work and built pens 6 by 12 feet, about three feet high, out of poles, then covered our tent clothes which makes it very comfortable. We cannot tell how long we may remain here. We can hear cannons and fire all day and all night. We are just 10 miles from Petersburg and 20 miles from Richmond.

Soon thereafter Samuel began to make requests of Silence for items he needed in Virginia:

October 11, 1864   Bermuda Hundred Near Point of Rocks #7

Silence, I want you to get me a pair of gloves, sheepskin or buckskin. Don't get very costly ones, and send them to me by mail. We cannot get them here for less than three dollars per pair—I think you can get them there for about $1.50.

It is likely that the evenings were beginning to become rather chilly at that time of the year in Virginia, thus the need for gloves. Still, one would think that the quartermaster would have provided gloves.

Since the soldiers were issued only one of some of these items each year, one can imagine the condition of those items after a number of months of use.

Samuel again made his request for gloves:

October 17, 1864   Bermuda Hundred   #8

I wrote you a letter some four days ago. I would like to have you send me a pair of sheepskin gloves lined with cotton flannel and send them by mail.

He began to make more requests of items from home as he settled in. He also described the prices of some goods in Virginia and also described the food they drew from their supply company:

October 23, 1864   Bermuda Hundred   #9

I wrote to Enoch [his brother-in-law, stationed with Company K, 150th Pennsylvania Volunteers in Washington, D.C.] *to send me one dollar's worth of postage, which he did. You spoke about how I liked woolen shirts. I like them very well. We have very good clothes, and warm. We drew our overcoats last week and gum blankets* [a black rubber coated canvas]. *They are nice on cool nights when we pitch our winter quarters . . . . I want you to send some apple butter and butter with Henry's folks. Butter is 80 cents per pound, sweet potatoes are 10 cents per pound, canned peaches $1.00 per can, onions 15 cents per pound, cheese 50 cents per pound and everything in proportion. We draw potatoes, beets, turnips, codfish, mackerel, fresh beef, salt beef and salt pork, coffee, sugar, bread and crackers, etc.*

Samuel soon made a request of Silence for a rather interesting type of medication, and also gave her some advice on support she might provide:

Silence, I want you to go to town and buy a box of Wrights Indian Vegetable pills and send them to me by mail. Just as soon as you receive this. We have a great deal of sickness in our regiment. There are about 25 in our company that [have] *the fever and ague. Mr. Blanchard is getting well fast, he is, so he can walk around the camp and do light work etc. Frank Hutchins is on the turn for the better with good care, and that he has, for he has a woman for a nurse. He is in the Sanitary Commission hospital. Silence, if you every have an opportunity of giving anything to the Sanitary* [Commission]*, I want you to do so, for I think it is one of the finest institutions that is in our army for the poor sick and wounded soldiers.*

Apparently, Samuel and many others during that period had a great deal of faith in the Wright's Indian Vegetable Pills. Darin Hayton, in an article posted October 18, 2009 on the website of the Philadelphia Area Center for History of Science, described these claims for the efficacy of Wright's Pills:

Wright's boldly listed the ailments cured by their vegetable pills. The laundry list of complaints included such standards as colds and coughs, fever and ague, and yellow fever. Alongside these stood more creative and ambitious claims: blotches on the skin, boils, dropsy, freckles, flatulency, gravel, neuralgia, pimples, and tumors.

One of the advertisements promised that the pill would "purify and circulate the blood." With the many illnesses of the soldiers, perhaps Samuel thought that taking those pills would prevent him from having those illnesses. Perhaps it worked, for he remained relatively healthy.

The United States Sanitary Commission was established in conjunction with the Federal Government in the North in June 1861, as a means of coordinating thousands of local relief agencies. The purpose of the Sanitary Commission was to supplement the government's war support by assembling food and medical supplies, providing nursing care and whatever other type of help was needed by the wounded soldiers. This group was initiated by women, and they were the main force behind all the other volunteer and aid organizations throughout the war.

This Commission went into the field, and inspected and improved sanitary conditions in the camps and hospitals. Their presence not only provided physical and emotional support for the troops, but also dramatically improved the cleanliness and orderliness of the camps and hospitals. It was headquartered in Washington, DC and had regional headquarters in ten Northern cities. Those regional office personnel helped in the creation of thousands of local capabilities. They were even involved in evacuating the wounded from the battlefield when there were no Army ambulances available, and provided places for the soldiers to stay when they were traveling to and from the field of battle.

In total, the Sanitary Commission contributed about $20 million in cash and supplies to the war effort, and countless volunteer days. (Wagner 661-662)

Samuel praised its work, as I am sure thousands of other soldiers did.

Samuel described to Silence a typical breakfast, and described some things he had to buy:

November 7, 1864   Butler Headquarters, eight miles in rear of
Bermuda Hundred   #12

This is Monday morning 7 o'clock. I just finished my breakfast. Presume you would like to know what I had. In the first place I had one pint of coffee and sugar enough to sweeten it; a piece of pork, two middling sized potatoes boiled; one loaf of light bread; salt and pepper.

We will probably not get any more pay for four months yet, then we expect six months' wages and one third more bounty, which in all will amount to $129. I intend to send home $100, the balance I intend to keep for spending money. I am running pretty short of money now, but will have what will last me some weeks. I have four dollars left. I do not buy much but what I am obligated to, etc. Everything is three times as high here as in the North or where you live. Writing paper is 25 cents a quire [a collection of 24 or sometimes 25 sheets of paper of the same size and quality: one twentieth of a ream]. Envelopes two *cents apiece—at them rates it wears away a few dollars of money. What used up my money so fast, I had to buy me a pair of boots, a gum blanket, suspenders, portfolio, ink stand, pens, etc. If you think of it when you write to me the next letter, put in a few dollars and I will pay you with good interest for it when I get home.*

Whether Samuel made good on that promise, we'll never know! In this letter, it seems he gave up on getting gloves from home.

You need not bother about them gloves. I can buy them here so that will save you the trouble, also save running the risk of them getting here.

It seems that Samuel collaborated with his fellow soldiers to get goods from home.

November 14, 1864   Bermuda Hundred   #14

John Henry is going to write home today also, and him and myself are going to have you and Mr. Koury's folks send us a lot of things in a box together. I want one quart of apple butter; two or three pounds of butter; two pounds of cheese; some apples if you choose; some honey if you please; one pound of fine cut tobacco. Tell Mr. Ewing I want the best. Mark my things that you send to me so we can tell them apart. Send just what you have a mind to and have Mr. Hervey to send them to the Christian Commission. (Wagner 662)

The Christian Commission played a very important part during the Civil War. The Christian Commission was founded by the Young Men's Christian Association, the well known YMCA, also in 1861, with a different but very important role in supporting the Union soldiers. In their case, they sent food and coffee wagons to the front. They also sent other useful supplies such as postage stamps and writing paper, the tools for making the all-essential contact with their loved one. At some camps, they set up reading rooms for the soldiers, which contained Bibles, magazines, newspapers and religious books. Their efforts were a nice supplement to the work of the Sanitary Commission, and provided $6 million to the war effort. (Wagner, 662).

As with the Sanitary Commission, the Christian Commission's efforts to aid the soldiers were very well received, as Samuel has indicated.

We do not have Silence's letters to Samuel, for he burned them to avoid their being taken by either the Confederates or someone else if he should be killed or wounded on the battlefield. We can infer from his letters the questions she had of him, in this case questions about where he slept, how he washed, and other aspects of his life as a soldier.

December 5, 1864   Headquarters Army of the Potomac   #17

Now you have asked me a few questions in regards to how we tent and wash, etc. Where we lay at present the shanties were built 7 by 10 feet, about 18 inches of ground dug out. First the timber built up the same as a log house and the cracks dabbed up. We use the ground for floor and generally 4 to 5 in a tent. They are very damp and dirty. We are also damp and dirty. A very bad place for a man to be sick. There are a great many in our company that have the ague. John Henry chills every other day, but does not want his folks to know, etc.

I do my own washing. We made wash boards. There are plenty [of] camp kettles in our company, that we can have at any time to heat our water, then we take a pork barrel and cut or saw it in two pieces, which makes very good tubs. Then we go in up to our elbows. Our shirts are easily washed but our drawers are cotton flannel, which gets very dirty . . . . I am glad you have sent me a pair of socks. The socks that I bought from home are good yet, but those I got from the government are about worn out. I don't need any undershirts, the weather is too warm. Oh, such lovely weather I never saw in my life. The roads are dusty.

Several months later, Samuel expressed the need for a new hat:

January 15, 1865   Headquarters Army of the Potomac   #23

I think you need not send me any more things, only one thing—and that is a hat. I want you to go to Mr. Ewing. Tell him to send me one by mail. I don't want a black one or a red one. Something like my old one I had. I don't want it to cost more than a couple of dollars, if you can get one for that. I cannot get one here for less than 6 or 7 dollars. Tell him to do it up in paper, send by mail and I will pay him when I come home. You can tell about the size by my old straw hat. Send it immediately, for I am as black as an Indian with my little blue cap on.

Samuel's letters about food, clothing and shelter during those first four months provides and interesting first-hand view of the life of a Civil War soldier.

Chapter 10

The Mounted Pioneer Corps:
Its Role and the Life of Its Soldiers

At the end of December 1864, Samuel's life in the military took a very favorable turn for him, and in many ways, ensured that he would survive the war. The choice he made many years earlier to choose cabinetry for a career was to pay off in ways he would never have expected. Here is his description of the major change:

December 28, 1864   *Army of the Potomac*   *#20*

Silence, I am not with my regiment any more. A week ago this morning, which is Wednesday, I was detailed by General Parks of the Ninth Army Corps of the Potomac to the Mounted Pioneer Corps. I will explain to you as well as I can what we have to do. In the first place, we have horses to ride wherever we go if not more than a mile. There are 25 men in the company. Wherever there is a bridge to build or repair, we have to do it, also go with the provisional train, help them through, fix bridges, etc. We carry no guns or arms of any kind, for we will not be placed in any danger of the enemy.

The work is middling hard, but what signifies work if a man is in safety. This is a permanent detail for one year or more. I am well-pleased with my position. The reason they detailed me was they wanted men that were steady and did not get drunk, etc. We just finished our cabin—and are in it. This evening is the first night.

I would have answered your letter before but had no chance for the other tents were so crowded that I could not write. I wrote two to you not more than ten days ago. I shall write to you often now, for when our

*day's work is done we have no more to do until the next day. We never
get up until seven o'clock. We also have a man to do our cooking. All
we do is to go to the cook shanty and get our plates and tin cups, get
our grub and then go to our tents, eat and carry our dishes back and
they are all washed and kept there until the next meal. We get soft
bread every day, roast beef, sometimes fried pork, also baked beans. I
have eaten my molasses and one can of apple butter. My butter, what I
kept, is done, but I have four pounds loaned that I shall get back again
in a few days.*

*The beauty of belonging to the Pioneer Corps is that you have no
luggage to carry. It is all hauled by our wagons that are in the corps. I
was chosen as an axeman. Some carry picks, some spades, etc.*

Before Samuel and others from the regiments of the Ninth Army
were chosen to be Mounted Pioneers, other types or organization had
attempted to do the work described by Samuel. Now that each corps had
its own Mounted Pioneer Corps, the commanding general had significant
flexibility and speed in using the mounted pioneers. As Samuel indicated,
he would not be in combat. However, other non-mounted pioneers were
not separated from their regiments, and they were very involved in
combat. In fact, they often had the highly dangerous role of crossing
enemy lines and destroying enemy fortifications to prepare the way for
the advance of the infantry regiments.

Samuel may have benefitted from circumstance in being assigned to the
Mounted Pioneers. According to Milo H. Miller, Samuel's son:

> *Arthur C. Huidekoper* [from a prominent family in Crawford County,
> Pennsylvania] *was Captain of Company A* [of the 211th regiment] *at
> the time and selected father for this service on account of his age (he
> was 42) and knowledge of carpentry and bridge building. This branch
> of the service would be termed engineering at present.* (Miller, *Ellis
> Family 115*)

In fact, Arthur C. Huidekoper was a captain in Company A, Samuel's
company, and also a native of Crawford County, Pennsylvania, so he
may even have known Samuel in Crawford County before the Civil
War, and surely would have seen Samuel work and seen his character

prior to recommending him to General Parke for a position as a Mounted Pioneer. He may very well have seen Samuel involved in cabinet-making in Crawford County, Pennsylvania. Too, he might have known that Samuel had been involved in bridge-building during his days of travels as a young man.

Another member of that family, Lt. Col. Henry Huidekoper, likely the brother of Arthur, was the head of the Pennsylvania 150th regiment. He was wounded at Gettysburg on July 1, 1863 and had an arm amputated, but stayed on in the service until early 1864. Alfred Huidekoper was a prominent citizen of Crawford County, as noted in Chapter 1.

Some of the work that Samuel had performed while in the regiment, but prior to his selection as a Mounted Pioneer, was similar to the work he would undertake in his new role:

October 27, 1964   Bermuda Hundred   #10

I am now on the detail duty chopping timber for hospitals, so if there is any fighting to be done I shan't be into it. We are about six miles from camp. I think it will take about three weeks. The work is very easy.

And also about that same time:

October 31, 1864   Camp Bermuda Hundred, Butler HQ   #11

" . . .myself and I.P. Kean were detailed to cut lumber for hospitals, which will probably take us three weeks . . ."

In the ensuing days, Samuel described more of the daily work of the Mounted Pioneers:

January 1, 1865   Headquarters Ninth Army Corps   #21

I will tell you that I am on guard watching our horses, that they do not kick each other or get untied and run about and tear up Ned. There are 41 head in all, in and about the stable. It requires two of us every night to stand guard or rather watch them. My turn comes every 11 or 12 nights. The balance of that time at nights I get my sleep. I think I have such a good place. I have no marching and nap sack to pack upon my back, or a gun to carry. Our luggage is all handled for us and we are on the horse's backs. I have a good horse, saddle and bridle and when we go and come from our work, we make our horses git. They are all fat and feel nice, etc. So be content. I think I was very lucky to get here. I presume it is all for the best, or at least I hope so.

Tonight it is very cold, freezing, the ground is white with snow but I am comfortable. I have a first rate warm shanty with a good fire place and a roaring big fire. My mess mates are fine men. Both from Pennsylvania. One is a young man. The other is married. Both were detailed the same time I was—one from my regiment, the other from the 208ᵗʰ regiment. All came out when we did. The single man's name is Huston and the other Bookhamer.

Fairly soon, Samuel began to appreciate even more the life of a Mounted Pioneer:

January 15, 1865   Headquarters Army of the Potomac   #23

As regards myself, my health is very good at present. In the first place I suppose I can prepare myself to answer some questions, which I will do willingly. The first question (in program you wanted to know) whether there is any church here. I am sorry to say there is none nearer than our regiment. Secondly, you wanted to know how far I was from the regiment [the 211ᵗʰ]. It is just about one mile. Thirdly and lastly, I get no more wages than I did when in the regiment. I am satisfied with my position, better than if I was getting twenty dollars a month. The work is harder. My souls, what signifies work when a man has a good horse to ride to and from his work. We never go to work until nine o'clock, or after, and then come in for dinner and then quit before sundown. Then all you have to do—feed your horse, eat your supper, set around your shanty and go to bed when you please.

I have not been out much last week to work. I stayed at camp and shaved shingles for the lieutenant's cabin. Do you see I am somewhat favored by being a mechanic. I am very well and hearty but cannot keep sleep all night.

For that time, at least, Samuel had a rather pleasant life as a Mounted Pioneer. The next letter described the nature of some of his work, and also told of, "when the cat is away, the mice will play!"

January 26, 1865   Headquarters 9ᵗʰ Army Corps   #25

I am still making shingles right by my shanty. I hardly ever go out with the boys to the woods or on the road to work. Our sergeant is going home this weekend on furlough. Then we will have a good time. I have a spirited horse, and a nice rider. He can jump a ditch or log just like a rabbit.

Although one might think of a war as constant battle, Samuel's letters show that when there were lulls in battles, things could be rather quiet and peaceful:

February 1, 1865   Headquarters 9ᵗʰ Army Corps   #26

We have not had much to do now, only chop wood and burn it. Our sergeant has gone home on furlough. So, we have a good time now, only lay around . . . . This Sunday 12 degrees and very windy and cold from the Northwest and we had to work all day making roads which went very much against my will, but what are we to do when we are ordered to work. I don't think we will have to answer for it in the day of Judgment. I hope you spent the Sabbath Day differently.

It was in this letter that he mentioned burning Silence's letters:

Your letters I have burnt them all, but if we stay in camp I shall save them until spring, when I will burn them. There is no one sees them for I keep them packed up in my portfolio but then I read them over two or three times then burn them.

Although Samuel did not want to work on the Sabbath, there were times when it was unavoidable:

February 11, 1865   Headquarters 9ᵗʰ Army Corps   #28

This evening I received your letters of the 3ʳᵈ and 5ᵗʰ which found me in good health and was much pleased to hear that you were all well.

I did not intend to answer this until tomorrow, but Colonel Pierce came home this, or rather back home from furlough. Coming from the station he observed several bad bridges, which he ordered repaired tomorrow. There we have got to work whenever the order is given. Although he is not a man than wants his man to work on the Sabbath Day, but the road is impassible for teams, where there are hundreds of them have to cross every day.

At about this time, Samuel described how some of the items shipped to him, and to others, were unfortunately diverted:

February 19, 1865   *Headquarters 9th Army Corps*   *#29*

Silence, I want you so ask someone who knows whether there is an Adams Express Office in Meadville, but I think that there is. I am not sure but you find out and let me know in your next letter. You wanted to know whether I wanted some more things sent in a box. I think it will hardly pay so late in the winter. There is no telling how long our corps may stay here. All the boxes that are sent to soldiers are opened and a great many things in the boxes are eaten by the poor swell head officers. I will tell you why they are opened. There is any amount of whiskey smuggled through to the soldiers of the army. There have been boxes come to our Pioneer Corps since I am in it, that has whiskey put into fruit cans and soldered up, so I think you need not send me any [boxes]. Save them until I get home and I will help you eat them. If you have a mind you may send me a pair of socks by mail and tell Mr. Buck not to charge so much postage as he did on the hat and gloves. He should not have charged more than 13 cents but I do not care. They suit me first rate and just the fit.

In that same letter, he described his work of that day:

We worked seven days last week and today is the Sabbath. We had our horses all saddled and mounted to go to work and were hitched, when Colonel Pierce told us we would not work today, so we put our horses in the stable again and took our axes and chopped pieces of wood for the old barn, which took us probably four hours.

At times the Mounted Pioneers had to work in very unpleasant weather:

March 23, 1865   Headquarters 9ᵗʰ Army Corps   #33

We have nice weather here. The apple trees are pretty near covered with leaves. The will bloom in a few days. Everything is growing in spite of the war. Today with the stormiest day I have ever seen. You could not see fifty rods for the sand. It blew a hurricane all day. We were in the woods cutting and splitting corduroy timber. We had to stop work for a while an account of too many trees falling. The pines in Virginia are very easily uprooted, the ground being so sandy.

Here Samuel makes reference to cutting "corduroy timber." His Mounted Pioneers had the very laborious task of building corduroy roads, which were roads made from timbers cut and laid across swampy, muddy and low areas to facilitate the movement of the troops, carriages and horses. These roads were temporary in nature, meant only for short term use in moving the army through wet, muddy terrain.

After the cessation of hostilities on April 9, 1865, there was still work to do for the Mounted Pioneers:

April 16, 1865 Burkville Station, Headquarters 9ᵗʰ Army Corps #38

This is the Lord's Day in the evening. I thought I would write you a few lines. I am very tired this evening after working hard all day cutting timber for repairing the roads which are in awful condition. The whole army, that is Potomac and James, are on their way towards Richmond and Petersburgh, City Point. Our corps remains here and along the South Side Railroad from this place to Petersburgh. I cannot tell you how long we may stay here, but I rather think not very much longer.

April 25, 1865   City Point, Virginia 9ᵗʰ Army Corps   #39

Our corps is all at Washington but one division and that is here waiting for boats. They are taking all their wagon trains, horses, mules and artillery and everything. I only hope we will be sent home, for I am

sick and tired of soldiering. We have nothing to do here, only take care
of the horses and eat and lay around in our tents.

The essence of the letters regarding the work of the Mounted Pioneers is that that corps played a critical role in providing the infrastructure to keep the Ninth Corps moving effectively. The fact that Samuel K. Miller was assigned to that special group enabled him to be safe for the last six months of his service in the Union Army.

Chapter 11

The Election of 1864:
Samuel's View of the Big Picture—
and the End

During the early part of Samuel's participation in the Union Army, the election of 1864 was looming, so it is interesting to see that upcoming election through his eyes.

As his regiment passed through Washington, DC on the way to the Petersburg, Virginia area, they participated in a march through that city. This was not an ordinary march:

> *October 11, 1864*   *Bermuda Hundred Near Point of Rocks*   *#7*
>
> *Today we vote for state officers. We had all our tickets sent us. Our regiment will most all go for the Republican ticket.*
>
> *I must tell you that when we started for this place, we marched through the city of Washington. There were two flags hanging across the street. The first one was a McClellan flag. When we came about to it, we sallied off to the left of it, and we all commenced groaning and hissing. Then we came to old Lincoln we marched right under it and cheered it very heartily. I tell you what a cheering there was for about a half hour, by the citizens as well as the soldier boys.*

I am not sure what the officers were thinking as the Union Army troops were breaking formation to do this jeering and cheering! It would have been a spectacle to witness.

Samuel wanted to be sure that he would have the opportunity to vote in that election:

October 11, 1864   Bermuda Hundred Near Point of Rocks   #7

Ask Doctor White how we are to get our tickets for the presidential election, whether they will be sent to us or not, or whether we will vote here. Tell him to give you some information about it.

Samuel's fellow soldiers in the 211th had high hopes about the potential results of the upcoming election:

October 23, 1864   Bermuda Hundred   #9

There is big excitement among the soldiers about the coming election. Old Abe is, I think, our president for four years more. The opinion is all through the army that this terrible rebellion will close by spring or sooner.

The excitement grew day by day leading up to the election:

November 7, 1864   Butler Headquarters   #12
Eight Miles in rear of Bermuda Hundred

Tomorrow is the day set for the great contest who shall be the president. Old Abe or Little Mack. I hope and pray Mack may be defeated. Our regiment will pretty much all go for Lincoln. I am little afraid that Lincoln will be licked. By the time you receive this letter I presume we will know who is the man that has the finishing of this war. I hope to God it may come to a close in two months so we may all return to homes and families and live a Christian life the balance of our days on Earth.

Here was his comment about the aftermath of the election:

I suppose you heard that General Sherman has burnt Atlanta. He is moving his army, that 70,000, upon Richmond. He has destroyed 30 miles of railroad and burns everything in his way and if our great commanders are not fooled, Richmond and Petersburgh must fall before many days. Praise to God for it. Lincoln is elected again without a doubt. Thank God he is—for this cruel war will soon be over.

Samuel's hopes, and those of his fellow soldiers, were boosted by Lincoln's reelection, but their hopes for an early end to the hostilities were premature.

Chapter 12

The Family and Community
at Home in Pennsylvania

In most wars, there are sharply varying sentiments about the purpose of the war, and therefore strong voices either in support of, or against, the involvement of the community in that war. That was the case in Samuel's home town of Hartstown and in Crawford County, Pennsylvania.

Some of the local newspapers had urged peace at any cost. *The Crawford Democrat,* a newspaper published in Meadville, Crawford County, Pennsylvania, from 1840 to 1884 seemed to publish only the letters from that point of view. For example, it publicized letters written to the paper from the soldiers from Crawford County who were off fighting for the Union, particularly those letters where the men stated they "just wanted to come home." The soldiers' letters included comments such as:

> *"I did not enlist to free the infernal Negroes."*
> *"We can never bring back the Union by fighting to free the Negroes."*
> *"Compromise on any possible terms."*

The *Crawford Democrat* insisted on June 16, 1863, that "the 'Butternuts' are willing to fight for Uncle Sam, but they are not inclined to fight for Uncle Sambo." The term "Butternut" came to be used as a synonym for the term "Copperhead." The Dictionary of American History provides a brief historical context for these terms.

> *On July 20, 1861, the term "Copperhead" appeared in the New York Tribune and within a year was widely employed to describe pejoratively both Democrats sympathetic to the South and all Democrats opposed to the war policy of President Abraham*

Lincoln. Literally, the word denotes a poisonous snake. Strongest in Ohio, Indiana and Illinois, the Copperheads, sometimes known as Butternuts or Peace Democrats, particularly objected to the Emancipation Proclamation because they completely rejected the idea of black equality and feared an influx of freed blacks into the northern states. Having fled Europe to avoid military service, some German-American and Irish-American Democrats vigorously objected to the military draft and engaged in antidraft riots in several northern cities, notably New York City. (Dictionary of American History)

An editor of the *Crawford Democrat* printed a letter from an angry soldier who declared his disillusionment after discovering the war was being waged to promote emancipation rather than to save the Union. He had hoped that Northerners would have enough courage to stand up for their rights and there would not be another draft in this war. As the war proceeded, however, the tone of the *Crawford Democrat* become more balanced, describing the events of the war, but not publicizing resistance against the efforts to save the Union.

By the end of the conflict, the *Crawford Democrat* praised the "epidomy (sic) of magnanimity" between Grant and Lee at the time of the surrender. The *Crawford Democrat* went through an interesting evolution over the four years of the war, finally being gracious to those two famous generals and implicitly accepting the fact that the Union forces had prevailed. (*Crawford Democrat*, April 1865.)

The Republicans labeled the Copperheads as traitors, while the Copperheads saw themselves quite differently. They felt they were patriotic, a loyal opposition which wanted to have the Union restored through negotiation rather than war. They felt that the war measures were unconstitutional, and they viewed the President's acts as tyrannical. As the war progressed, President Lincoln was reelected and the Union Army won some important battles, the influence of the Copperheads began to fade.

Nevertheless, Samuel was returning to a town whose citizens had been told for several years by its newspapers that the war was not worth the fight. What was left of those sentiments?

After the events at Fort Sumter, it did not take long for Crawford County, Pennsylvania to react with indignation. Very soon after the word got out to all the towns of that part of the State, groups of citizens met and passed resolutions supporting the Union in its response. The action taken by the citizens of Meadville, the county seat, provide a good insight into the feelings that prevailed throughout the country during those critical years, particularly as the events began to unfold in 1861. Everyone realized that that was a critical time for the country, because it could become permanently divided. President Lincoln called for 75,000 volunteers, to be raised as soon as possible.

With the challenge of the loss of union, people of all political persuasion put aside their differences and met at the Court House in Meadville on three consecutive evenings, Thursday, Friday and Saturday, April 18, 19, and 20 of 1861. All assembled agreed on the need to stand by the Union and support it in any way possible. A committee was established to deal with raising a Meadville company of volunteers, and to help all the families of those who might volunteer. That committee passed the following resolution:

> *Resolved: That for the purpose of showing the loyalty and patriotism of our entire people, the occupants of every house in this place and community be requested to display the Stars and Stripes.* (Bates I 344)

Just after the three-evening sessions, a large group gathered with very short notice at the Court House again on April 22, 1861. Those assembled wanted to show that they were very supportive of the Government. Judge Derickson of Meadville was the spokesperson, and he defined the purpose of that meeting. He spoke of the importance of supporting the American flag and the Constitution. He emphasized strongly that this was not a political issue, rather, that a Republican government can be maintained. A committee was then formed to gather the feelings of the people. One very important clause was:

> *Resolved: That we are neither Democrats or Republicans, but friends of our country, and that those who attempt to prostitute party names to disguise their treason, while rebels tear down the American flag, are, nevertheless, traitors who will be shunned by patriots and*

denounced and disowned by their own posterity, as were the Tories of the Revolution, against whose doubly-damned memories, the slow finger of scorn will be pointed in all coming time. (345)

With this resolution, it was pretty clear that the local leaders in Crawford County intended to brand anyone who opposed the saving of the Union as traitors, "Tories," a very harsh term. Would that have set the stage for harsh treatment, or just shunning, for some of the local people who proudly proclaimed that they were "Copperheads." The reaction to that resolution was quite dramatic. At the April 22 meeting, a committee was named to obtain names as volunteers. There was great enthusiasm during the meeting, and it adjourned with "three cheers for the Union" and "three cheers for the Stars and Stripes.

Daily life in Meadville was transformed; a high pitch of excitement created energy that surged throughout the community. Those who lived in the community experienced a level of excitement they had never experienced in their lifetimes. Volunteers soon to be sent off to battle were drilling and marching through the streets, bands were playing and the American flag was displayed everywhere, far more than usual. Everyone in Meadville and the surrounding areas was talking about the war. Before the end of April, to the approval of the Governor of Pennsylvania, five companies were raised and ready to leave. One of the five companies consisted of 78 men from Allegheny College, which is located in Meadville. The spirit to serve obviously spilled into the ranks of the college students!

For one of the five companies, Captain Johnson's, over $3,000 was raised to outfit his company and to help the families of those who had volunteered. His company left for Pittsburgh on May 2, 1861, a very fast response of about three weeks from when the word reached Meadville about Fort Sumter. When that company left, the whole town was there to send them off. That large crowd was charged with enthusiasm, they called out cheers, sang and gave their heartfelt prayers. The company moved off in their vehicles for the intermediate stop in Linesville, also in Crawford County, on their way to Pittsburgh.

Over $3,000 were raised in Meadville to fit out Capt. Johnson's company, and to assist the families of the volunteers. This command left

Meadville for Pittsburgh May 2, 1861. The whole town turned out to greet their departure, and the scene was one of the wildest enthusiasm, cheers and heart felt prayers mingling together, as the vehicles which carried the command to Linesville left the camp ground. (Ibid)

It is not likely that the feelings of support for the Union were always held at such a high pitch of excitement as they were at the beginning of the War. It is, however, very likely that this great reservoir of support was well maintained throughout the Civil War, and for the most part, greatly overshadowed the role of the press and those who wanted peace, virtually at any cost.

The Heidekoper family participated actively in these events, and one of those who drafted that resolution was Alfred Huidekoper. The Huidekopers were a prominent family in this community, and Samuel's life was impacted, both directly and indirectly by them. Arthur C. Huidekoper was an officer in Samuel's regiment, primarily serving as a lieutenant, and was promoted to Captain at the end of the hostilities on April 10, 1865. Lieutenant Arthur Huidekoper was instrumental in recommending that Samuel K. Miller be taken from the ranks of the 211th Pennsylvania Infantry and assigned to the Mounted Pioneer Corps of the Union Ninth Corps.

The Huidekopers had been influential leaders in Meadville since 1804. In that year Harm Jan Huidekoper, who had been born in the Netherlands in 1776, moved to Meadville as the agent for the Holland Land Company. The purpose of his company was to acquire land in New York State and Western Pennsylvania. At that time, Meadville was a village of about 25 or 30 houses and a population of 150. Harm Jan Huidekoper, after effectively reorganizing the management of the land for the Holland Land Company, eventually purchased a significant amount of land in Erie, Crawford, Warren, and Venango Counties. In time, several of Harm Jan Huidekoper's grandsons responded to the call to support the Union very early, and throughout the war.

Henry S. Huidekoper was the most prominent of that family who participated in the Civil War. He graduated from Harvard College and ultimately became a general in the Union Army and received the highest decoration for bravery, the Medal of Honor. While in command of the

150th Pennsylvania Infantry at Gettysburg on July 1, 1863, he was wounded twice, losing his right arm. According to the citation, "while engaged in repelling an attack of the enemy, he received a severe wound of the right arm, but instead of retiring remained at the front in command of the regiment." Henry S. Huidekoper had a very illustrious career after his participation in the Civil War.

Other members of the Huidekoper family were instrumental in the civic life of Meadville during the Civil War and for many years following.

Perhaps, like many other men who left behind families as they entered the military in the Civil War, Samuel continuously had in mind the welfare of his family back in the small town of Hartstown, Crawford County, Pennsylvania. His letters to his wife show how he endeavored to work with her to keep the family in good care, good health and good spirits when he was away.

Samuel was to receive a bounty of $500 for his part in filling the Turnersville quota. Those funds were to be deposited with Benoni Ewing, who kept the store in Hartstown during the war, and there Silence made her purchases for the family. That, it seems, was a rather novel way of providing for his family while he served in Virginia, perhaps ensuring that his family would be well provided for and without his wife having to keep the money at their home. The $500 was not all paid at one time; it was paid in segments, the last of which was paid when he was mustered out.

From his first letters, one sees his effort to ensure that his family was being cared for:

> *September 9, 1864   Camp Reynolds [11 miles from Pittsburgh] #1*
>
> *Silence, I hope you are reconciled by this time. Keep in good spirits and try and get along the best you can until I return again, which I certainly will do. Don't starve yourself and children and go respectable in society. Your money lays at your command. Use what you want. I did not see Plum Hagen, but get it and use it for your debts.*

Silence apparently qualified to get some relief funds because Samuel would be serving in the Union Army:

September 12, 1864   Camp Reynolds   #1

That paper you got at the commissioners, take it to Esys Henry or Gordon and have it filled out so you can draw your relief money.

No doubt there were a myriad of details running through Samuel's mind pertaining to the management of their home in Hartstown:

October 3, 1864   Bermuda Hundred   #5

I hope you and the children are well and getting along well. Don't forget those apple trees, the 31st of this month, and have them set right and keep the cow off of the lot.

October 11, 1864   Bermuda Hundred Near Point of Rocks   #7

I wish you had sent for the Certificate [possibly to get relief funds] a few days sooner. I am afraid you will not get this in time to do you any good. I would have sent one to you long ago but they told us I did not need anything of the kind, that you could draw your money without it. I should of got this at Provost's office in Meadville. But there was so much said concerning it that we did not know what to do, but I got one from our Captain this morning, if it is good for anything. Why, alright, and if not why, I do not know how to work it.

It must have been frustrating to be at such a distance and not know the procedures for making this arrangement regarding the payment of relief monies.

Sometimes it was necessary for Silence to make some larger purchases. Samuel seems to provide assurances for her that she was capable of making good decisions about those matters:

November 7, 1864   Butler Headquarters,
Eight Miles in rear of Bermuda Hundred   #12

You also requested me to say or give my consent whether you should buy that stove from Manning. I am very willing that you should get it. I think it is very cheap at four dollars. I am perfectly willing for you to

*use all the money you want to make you and the children comfortable.
I am not afraid of you going beyond anything, only what you necessary
want to use judgment and economy, that is all I want, and I know you
have never done anything else since we were married. Therefore, the
money I left you lays at your command, and as regards myself, I am to
expend whatever for clothing or victuals, only paper, ink and stamps
and envelopes (tobacco, of course).*

Samuel was naturally concerned about the kind of help that Silence
should have at home to manage all the work at the house, as well as
taking care of the boys:

November 23, 2864   Camp Bermuda Hundred   #14

*You wanted to know of me if I was willing that you should keep Mary
Davis for company this winter. Yes, if she will stay, keep her, for she
is company for you. I don't think you can get anyone that will suit you
any better in the country. I am perfectly willing to have you keep her.*

*You said that you had got that stove. Now you want new pipe. Go to the
Masons and get all you want and be careful that you make it very safe
up stairs in the chimney that there will be no danger of fire. I have never
thought at any time to write to you about my shop, whether the neighbors
bother you about the tools, etc. Don't let them carry them off.*

I am very glad that you can get your relief money.

Whatever the amount of the relief money, it was sure to help. Samuel
had good reason for being concerned about his tools, for that was his
livelihood!

Despite the distance between Samuel and Silence, they had many
discussions in their letters about home management concerns such as
money and the preservation of food:

December 14, 1864 Army of the Potomac, Petersburgh, Virginia #18

*I am glad that you have your potatoes dug and the cave fixed—so they
will keep. How many bushels did you have? You need not send me any*

money. I sold my boots for six dollars, and that will last me until we get our pay. I think by the first of the next month we will get our pay. I am glad that you have got part of your relief money. I was afraid that you would not get it at all. I presume it is very acceptable to you if it is in small dribs. How will the hay hold out? Will you have enough?

By early February, Samuel had begun to think about what he will do with their house when he returns home:

February 1, 1865   Headquarters 9th Army Corps   #26

Silence, have you your stove set up in the room yet? Silence, I want to have five hundred dollars in money when I get home. I want to finish my house and dig a cellar, and buy some hardware at Pittsburgh when I come and some groceries, too.

Soon it was clear that Silence would be receiving the relief money:

February 9, 1865   Headquarters 9th Army Corps   #27

You say you received five dollars more of relief money. You say it seemed like a gain. I think so myself, and a considerable gain. If I do pay a certain portion by tax, I don't think I have to pay 50 cents a year toward it. Did not you say that you lost two months pay in the start? You ought to have had pay for five months, which would make 25 dollars. It does not matter much either way. All I have to say, take all you can get. I think I am entitled to it.

It seems that Silence was considering taking in boarders to help with her finances. Here is Samuel's response:

February 11, 1865   Headquarters 9th Army Corps   #28

You had better not take in any boarders, I will give you my reasons why. Not that I fear it would raise a talk, or anything of that kind, but I don't think it would pay, for everything is high, and too much trouble for a woman in seeing to get provisions. Furthermore, we are not prepared with bedding, etc. Tell Abner [her brother] for him to board them. He may need a little money to buy his wife a cloak. Silence, if you hear of a chance to bargain with some of the old women in the country for goose feathers, do it. Tell them to have them ready for you by fall coming. I think, then, feathers will be cheap.

A few words of advice concerning a cow they were to receive, and some comments on the "boys" in Hartstown:

March 23, 1865   Headquarters 9th Army Corps   #33

Silence, I suppose sugar making is over any day. If you get a chance to buy some at a reasonable price, buy some, but I presume store sugar is about as cheap as home made. You wanted to know when our cow would come in. I drove her to McMaster's I think the last day of June. Bill Andrews went with me and then went home from there to the picnic at the McMichael's. I think you will find it marked in one of the almanacs. She ought to come in the first of next month.

Where does those men that have sold their farms intend doing? Go west or buy again in the neighborhood? I think the boys had better hold onto their farms for they cannot better themselves, not about there. What did they ever do with Alfreda [Silence's sister] *about her claim. Did she ever send them a deed? If mother wants to come and live with us, take her. Tell the boys not to run away. Stand the draft and if any of them are drafted to come, there will not be much fighting done.*

Payments to Samuel were erratic, and that put a strain on their finances. After an initial payment of $133.33 on September 17, very early in time of service, he was not paid again until March 2, 1865. At one point, he had to "dun" Silence for some money, so she sent him $5. He seemed seldom to have $7 or $8, often not that much. In the end, according to Milo's record, Samuel received $156.29 for his service, in addition to the $500 bounty.

These are just some examples of the interchange between Samuel and Silence that dealt with the many issues left to Silence to handle when Samuel went off to war, his advice and comments, and his concerns about the well being of Silence and the two little boys, Myron and Milo.

Chapter 13

The Copperheads and Resistance to the Draft

In his letters, Samuel makes references to the "Copperheads" back in his home town of Hartstown, Pennsylvania.

Throughout the war, the Peace Democrats had to defend themselves against charges of disloyalty. Because the Copperheads did not volunteer and were vocal about their resistance to the draft and to the war, it is easy to imagine how those serving with the Union Army felt about those at home who were opposed to what they were doing to preserve the Union. There was always the threat of the Copperheads being drafted if their district did not meet its quota. In a number of not-so-subtle ways, the Copperheads showed their defiance.

As stated earlier, there was strong resistance to the draft. The Civil War was the first real effort on the part of the federal government to draft men into the armed forces. Both the North and the South used the draft, or at least the threat of a draft, to muster men into the service. Some strongly favored the draft, others hated it. Draft riots occurred in 1863, with one particularly chilling episode in New York City. Because the men had the option to volunteer and be paid a bounty for entering the service, a very low percentage of men were actually drafted.

In Samuel's home state of Pennsylvania, there was significant opposition to the war and to the draft. By 1863, the morale in the North was low because of the Conscription Act of 1863, the defeats that had been incurred in battles, mounting casualties, and for some, the impact of the Emancipation Proclamation, announced in that year. "While emancipation was noble, widespread racism enraged many who denounced the 'war to free negroes.'" Federal authorities had to deal with the increasing opposition to the war and in particular, to the draft. Draft resistance in the State of Pennsylvania was widespread. The authorities faced lying and even violence.

The most challenging areas were in the rural areas, where there was significant poverty and ethnic minorities, such as the Irish miners in the anthracite coal mining area in the northern part of the state. Other groups strongly opposed to the draft were the German-speaking farmers and tradesmen in the central part of the state, those areas where the German immigrants had settled in the early 1700s. There were also what might be considered the mountain people, tough people who lived in the Appalachian mountains in the western part of the state. The mountains in the northern part of the state were considered "deserter country." In 1864, the military sent expeditions to those area and arrested many who had evaded the draft. (Pennsylvania Civil War 150)

Despite the strong resistance to the war and the draft in parts of Pennsylvania, the state had the second highest enlistment of soldiers in the war, totaling over 340,000. Although they served in segregated units, 8,600 black soldiers served in 11 Pennsylvania regiments. More than 33,000 Pennsylvanians died in the service and many thousands more were wounded. (Ibid)

With that background on the Copperheads and the resistance to the draft, how did the dislike of the Copperheads manifest itself in Samuel's letters? In his letter of January 8, 1865, quoted earlier in Chapter 4, Samuel had made reference to some of the men in Hartstown who might be considering going to Canada to escape the draft. In this same letter, he went on to say:

January 8, 1865   *Headquarters Army of the Potomac*   *#22*

I would like to talk to some of them Copperheads. I think I could tell them some things that would not set very well in their stomachs.

We can only speculate as to what Samuel may have said to those men when he encountered them in that small town when he returned!

Samuel wanted to know what was happening with some of the fellows in Hartstown regarding the draft status, and also what the entire township's plans may be:

> *February 9, 1865   Headquarters 9th Army Corps   #27*
>
> *Let me know about whether Findlay McQuiston was enrolled in the draft and what the Township intends doing in regards to filling their quota.*

As the war proceeds, one can sense Samuel's bitterness toward the Copperheads, who had avoided being involved in the conflict:

> *February 26   Headquarters 9th Army Corps   #30*
>
> *You can tell the Copperheads that the day is ours, and we do not thank them, either, for their assistance.*

In a subsequent letter, he referred to specific people whom he directly or indirectly identified as Copperheads:

> *March 30, 1865   Headquarters 9th Army Corps   #35*
>
> *How does Ellen Johnson feel about Charley being drafted? Ben sent me a list of five townships. I see that Andrew I. Galbreath is one on the list. James C. Hart, Bill McLenahan. Oh, but I think that is good for him, the poor, mean Copperhead. It is all good or those Secesh* he name given to those who favored the Secession]. *It had ought to of hit George MLenahan and Plum Heagen. They may not see any fighting, for the General and other officers say it will wind up in about 60 days.*

In one of his final letters, he made his last comment about the Copperheads:

> *May 14, 1865   Alexandria, Virginia   #44*
>
> *Let me know in your next letter how the Copperheads seem to feel about the assassination of President Lincoln. The Copperheads here dare not chirp or say anything disloyal in regard to it.*

Knowing Samuel's strong feelings against the Copperheads, we can only speculate about the relationships in Hartstown, and other communities, when he returned to civilian life in his town of about 200 people and brushed shoulders with those men in their daily lives.

Chapter 14

Hope for the End of the War

By the latter part of 1864, the men in Samuel's unit were becoming more hopeful that the end was in sight:

December 28, 1864   Army of the Potomac   *#20*

We all think of coming home by the first of May. The war is playing out. You would think so if you were here and see the Johnnies coming in every morning. Sherman has whipped them all out in Georgia. They all say there is no use to fight any more with the North. They also have sent peace men to Washington for peace. I hope and pray it may close tomorrow.

January 1, 1865   Headquarters Army of the Potomac   *#21*

If old Ben ever asks you anything about me, tell him that we are going to put an end to this Rebellion by spring. All we ask is for Sherman to clean them out in Georgia and old U.S. Grant and his army hold the Rebs here in Richmond. By next spring they will all desert. They only come at the rate of 20 and 25 a night to our headquarters, besides what comes in at other places all across the lines, a distance of about 110 miles.

There were always hopes that a peace settlement could be achieved:

February 1, 1865   Headquarters Army of the Potomac   #26

There is strong talk of a peace settlement. May God grant it may be so. Vice President Stephans Hunter and Campbell are at Washington to see whether there is hope for peace. They came across the picket line opposite Petersburgh and were escorted by General Parks in a four-horse carriage into Meade's station where they took the cars for

City Point, thence by water to Washington. If they do come to any terms of peace, the war will end in a couple of months. Then, in all probability, us new troops will be home by the end of May. You can tell the people if they doubt this news, tell them it is so far there was one of our boys saw the men who come to Meade's station. Troops are all anxious to hear of peace once more. I say Amen to that!

The end seemed to be near as the tempo of the war increased:

February 26, 1865   Headquarters 9ᵗʰ Army Corps   #30

Today everything is in commotion. The soldiers all seem to feel rejoiced to death to hear of the constant good news that comes to headquarters of the Rebellion coming to a close. It certainly is cheering news indeed to hear of General Sherman's success in the South. There is also a strong rumor that the Rebs are evacuating Petersburgh. If not, there are strong movements going on. They burned their factories last evening about dusk, and a number of other buildings. Grant ordered our Battery men to open a few shots to see whether they are about to evacuate that place but it seems they still occupy the place or at least they replied pretty lively. But deserters say they are evacuating the place as fast as they possibly can. You can tell the Copperheads that the day is ours, and we do not thank them, either for their assistance.

The Johnnies came to our lines at an average rate of five hundred per days. Forty six reported here at Headquarters this morning, 35 yesterday. Remember, these only came in on the line of the 9ᵗʰ Corps. On the Army of the James, they number about one hundred per night. They all say the thing is played out. They also say that their leading commanders promised them to not desert until the 4ᵗʰ of March, but they found out differently by their own good learning. Instead of being sent home they were preparing themselves for a big battle. That is why they desert so. Old Lee is making another move somewhere, but Old Grant is waiting. I would not be at all surprised if we were in Petersburgh next Sunday. That is the supposition by almost every one. I hope the thing will soon close.

Give Doctor White my respects. Tell him for me—that the Rebs are a badly whipped nation. We all want to be home by July 4. Send on your Valentines. There will be no danger of them ever getting into battle.

March 11, 1865   Headquarters 9ᵗʰ Army Corps   #32

Our army is filling up every day. There are trainloads arriving, filling old regiments, also a number of new regiments. There are three new regiments laying in the woods about one hundred rods in our rear. They are playing some beautiful pieces on the band. The whole army is in commotion for the last ten days. Grant is making the preparations for a big Battle. All the old soldiers say they never saw such a move as this is going to be. The intention is as near as I can learn, the three corps laying on our left, the 2ⁿᵈ, 5ᵗʰ and 6ᵗʰ are to move and form a junction with Sherman. Scofield in the South and Sheridan with the cavalry on the West, Grant with the 9ᵗʰ Corps to hold this place.

We do not move for some time unless the Rebs are whipped and evacuate Petersburgh and Richmond.

It is quite surprising that Samuel K. Miller, a private, would have such information about the intentions of the Union Army's plans!

More talk of peace:

March 23, 1865   Headquarters 9ᵗʰ Army Corps   #33

The Rebs talk strong of making peace. You ought to read the papers and hear what they have to say. There were 40 came to our lines yesterday and today, that is just to our corps. I have prophesied all winter that the war would be closed this spring, I cannot think anything else. I feel like it hard and can't give it up.

We have not moved our headquarters yet. We may not have to move yet for several months.

With all the anticipation of when the war might end, a peace settlement achieved, the anxieties were surely increasing by the day. Clearly the forces were massing for what was intended to put an end to the war, so those forces—the "commotion"—were giving hope to Samuel and his fellow soldiers.

Chapter 15

The Last Days of the Campaign

Samuel described those final critical days of the Civil War in the Petersburg-Richmond campaign, then the calm after the end at Appomattox.:

March 30, 1865   Headquarters 9ᵗʰ Army Corps   #35

Last night and today all day it has rained steadily, which makes it disagreeable for Grant's army to march and fight. He moved yesterday morning about daylight from here with General Sheridan's and General Craig's entire force of cavalry beside part of five corps of infantry on our left to make a death blow of the Rebellion. Last night at about half past 10 o'clock, the Rebels massed troops in front of Petersburgh, but was unsuccessful in making the attack. They were received with a warm reception from our batteries, which opened up on them. I never saw such cannon. You would have thought all the stars in the heavens were falling. The night was dark and every shell that was thrown looked like a star shooting until it burst, which would make a large flash of light.

It will clear off. It has commenced to thunder. We are not at work today. The weather is very warm. We can work all day without our blouses or vests on.

Samuel did not write for over a week. This is not surprising considering the intensity of the war during those critical days. The next letter gives his summary of those recent days:

April 8, 1865   Headquarters 9th Army Corps   #36

I suppose you would like to hear from me. By this time I suppose you have heard that Peterburgh and Richmond belong to the Yanks, also the South Side Railroad, with forty-five thousand prisoners, eight generals, and driving the Rebs like chaff before the wind. General Lee's army is reduced down to 18,000. The rumor is that Grant gave Lee twelve hours to surrender. If not, the Ball goes on. We left our old camp last Monday morning, the 3rd, for the march. We followed the South Side Railroad all the way, a distance of forty-four miles. I think we will stop at Burkesville for a while, which is the junction of the Danville and Richmond. The darkies are tickled almost to death to see the Yanks.

You cannot expect to hear much from me at this time, only I am well and hearty. You can hear more at home of this campaign than I can write at present. I am writing this in our wagon. Don't get uneasy about me if you do not hear from me again in two weeks. The thing is going well. The war is coming to a close fast. I think by next week we will close the fighting.

My regiment [the 211th Pennsylvania] was in all the fight last Saturday. Sunday my company lost thirteen killed, wounded and missing. Captain Lee was killed, Isaac Graffis missing, also Selkirk Wade. The regiment lost heavy. The fighting was desperate. I saw them fight, make charges. Oh, such a contest I never saw. You will see all the news in the papers. We had pretty hard work on this march. I did not mind that we could ride. I will wait until evening. I may get a letter from you. I hope you are well.

We may all be home before a great while. Don't be alarmed about me, for I think I have a good position . . . .The Yanks are happy, are all eager to close the Rebellion. We live fine. We have hogs, sheep, turkeys, chickens and everything the country affords. Such a destruction of property. Buildings burned and furniture destroyed. I shall tell you about the raid when I come home.

Later, in a letter to his cousin Margarette Wills (who with her husband owned the Globe Hotel in Gettysburg at the time of the battle) in York, Pennsylvania:

Hartstown, Pennsylvania   *May 11, 1887*

I helped to take Petersburgh and Richmond and was within a few miles when Lee surrendered to Grant. I saw General Lee. He was a nice brave looking man. I saw Grant also, and all the generals. I also saw Lincoln a few days before he was killed up to Petersburgh on Monday afternoon after the fall of Petersburgh.

(The original of that letter is in the archives of Historic New Harmony, Incorporated, New Harmony, Indiana).

The following week was full of historic events, with the surrender at Appomattox and the assassination of President, as described in Samuel's next letter. The initial reaction by the Union soldiers was that the Confederates had killed Lincoln:

April 16, 1865   Burkville Station, Headquarters 9th Army Corps #38

This is the Lord's day in the evening. I thought I would write you a few lines. I am very tired this evening after working hard all day cutting timber for repairing the roads which are in awful condition. The whole army, that is Potomac and James, are on their way toward Richmond and Petersburgh, City Point. Our corps remains here and along the South Side Railroad from this place to Petersburgh. I cannot tell you how long we must stay here, but I rather think not very much longer.

I suppose you will hear of the murder of Lincoln before this reaches you and all the particulars, also about the assassination of Secretary Steward. I have not heard anything for ten years that has hurt my feelings so much as the murder of those men, but I presume it was the Lord's will they should die. He was killed by a confounded Rebel, which I presume in all probability was bribed to do the deed. Oh, what a wicked man he must be. Hanging is too good for him. The soldiers all swear vengeance against the Rebs. The Rebs that Lee surrendered are all running about at large. I can see hundreds of them every day, mostly dirty, thieving set of fellows, but they are watched very closely by our troops so they do not do any mischief to the Railroads.

I suppose there was some cannonading in Hartstown and other places when they got the news that Lee had surrendered his army. I heard today that Joe Johnson had surrendered his army, but it is not official but he will before a great while. I hope he will surrender so we can get home by harvest.

By the time of his next letter, Samuel was at City Point, on his way to Washington:

April 25, 1865   City Point, Virginia 9th Army Corps   #39

We landed here a couple of days ago, and are waiting hourly for transportation for Washington. My regiment [211th Pennsylvania] is at Washington now. What the Government intends doing with us, we have not yet learned. There are rumors in circulation that the 9th Corps is to be disbanded and sent home for sixty days. If not wanted at that time, to be discharged and sent home. Some say we are going to Texas and others say we are going to North Carolina.

Our corps is all at Washington but one division and that is here waiting for boats. They are taking all their wagon trains, horses, mules and artillery and everything. I only hope we will be sent home, for I am sick and tired of soldiering. We have nothing to do here, only take care of our horses and eat and lay around our tents. Mercy, but it is hot today!

Rather than being sent directly to Washington, he was sent to Alexandria, Virginia. Little did I realize when I lived in Alexandria from 1983 until 1988 that my great grandfather had spent the last days of his service in that area!

At that time, the rumors were flying:

April 30, 1865 Headquarters 9th Army Corps Alexandria, Virginia #40

We are laying one mile and a half from Alexandria. We arrived here yesterday morning about sunrise. My regiment is in sight from where we lay. They are all in good spirits of a speedy discharge. I think myself that we will be sent to our respective states this week. We may not get home for two weeks or not until the first of June. The war is over. Johnson has surrendered his army to Sherman. Kirby Smith has surrendered also. The War Department has stopped the purchase of all supplies, also the buying of horses, mules, cattle, only for the regular army. I have not been to Washington, yet I would like to go to see the boys [of the 211th], but I presume that we will stop there long enough so I can go to see them.

May 2, 1865   Headquarters 9th Army Corps Alexandria, Virginia #41

You said you thought that the war was about over. Yes, the great conflict has come to a close and our country is once more restored to peace and happiness and the fiendish enemy are getting their just dues. Wherever there are any, they are shot down like brutes in the forest. A man is not allowed to speak any disloyal sentiments whatever. If he does, he is shot or in other ways seriously punished, which is right. George McLenahan and some others that are rank Secesh would not fare very well here if they talk as they did when I was home.

I presume that you have heard that Booth has been captured and shot. His body no one knows where it is. The paper stated that it was thrown into the bottom of the Potomac River. We also heard that Jeff Davis has been killed. He was killed by his own men. He well deserved killing or something as bad. The Government is discharging District troops, now all Pennsylvania troops will be sent to their respective states, there to be discharged as fast as possible in order to reduce the recent expenses to one fourth by the first of June.

With time on his hands in and near Alexandria, he had time to reflect on his recent experiences and the deep feelings toward those affected by the war:

May 4, 1865   Headquarters 9th Army Corps Alexandria, Virginia #42

I feel happy to think that the war is at a close. I also feel sad and shed tears to read about those poor rebels and blacks—how rejoiced they are to be liberated from bondage. The playing of a band of musicians makes me shed tears. It seems that my heart is completely broken. The boys all say I am so quiet. I cannot help it. I feel so.

May it be the Lord's will that we may all safely return to our respective homes where we may forever worship Him, that is ever watchful over us. Silence, don't neglect to pray me, for I know you are a Christian and how wicked I have been that I was not one also—but if God spares my life I shall be one, too. I feel happy all the time, but feel I am still in darkness.

We still have our horses to take care of. We may have to turn them over in a few days and we may stay with them until our regiment is sent home. Then, of course, we shall have to go long. We have nothing to do at all, only take care of our horses and eat, but lying on the ground uses me up. It gives me a back ache some nights, so that in the morning I can scarcely get up.

Sherman's army is coming to Alexandria, then the two armies are to have a grand review. The War Department has ordered six hundred thousand discharges printed immediately. All citizen enlistees are to be discharged. It may take to the first of June before they get entirely hrough discharging all the armies.

I was down to Washington today with the sergeant and one of the boys out of the Pioneer Corps with a team to get a few things for Lieutenant Pierce, but did not have time to go to see the boys. [In this case, I believe he was talking about his brothers-in-law, Enoch and Benjamin Ellis, who were with Company K of the 150th Pennsylvania]. *I was within a short distance of the White House, too, but could not leave to see them. Everything seems to move briskly.*

The talk is now that the Ninth Corps will be one of the first corps discharged. We are all getting tired to death of laying about doing nothing. Not enough to digest our food. We have turned in our horses and equipment, so you see we have not even our horses to take care of. I wish they would send us to our regiments.

A grand parade was being scheduled for mid-June in Washington, D.C.:

May 14, 1865   Alexandria, Virginia   *#44*

There will be a general review of the whole army in Washington. Just as soon as Sherman's troops reach this point, that will be probably next Wednesday, the 17th, which will take two or three days. Then, the War Department intends to pay the army and discharge them as fast as they can.

Today's papers have the glorious news of the capture of Jeff Davis and his whole gang. He was captured at Irvinsville, Georgia. In all probability he will be hung by the neck. I think he deserves a severe punishment for he has been the great cause of all this dreadful carnage in our country and so much loss of blood and the cause of many a fatherless child, and caused many a widow. By reading the newspapers you will see the particulars of Jeff's capture and what they intend doing with the old chap.

The grand review in Washington was delayed until May 23 and 24, 1865:

May 21, 1865   Alexandria, Virginia #45

Next Tuesday and Wednesday is set apart for the final review, 23rd and 24th. The armies are to march in company front up Pennsylvania Avenue from the Capitol to the White House, thence to their respective camps again in light marching order without knapsacks. Immediately after the review we will return to our states to be discharged, which will probably take a week or ten days, not more than that as the furtherest.

I don't think I will be in the review unless we are sent to our regiments tomorrow or Monday. I will know in a day or two what they will do with us. You need not look for me until you hear me at the gate and whistle.

May 24, 1865   Alexandria, Virginia #46

I was not up to Washington to see the review. I need not tell you for why. You know that I do not care much for such things. [His last letter while in service]

Chapter 16

Samuel's Growth in Faith

To understand the context of the religious references in Samuel's letters, it is important to know his church affiliation in Pennsylvania. Largely influenced by his wife Silence Ford Ellis, he was a member of the Free Will Baptist Church of Adamsville, Crawford County, Pennsylvania. Her parents, John and Susan Ann Ellis, had been members of the Free Will Baptist Church in Mayfield, Maine from 1831 until their departure for Pennsylvania in 1841. It was clear from Chapter 3 that John Ellis was an abolitionist, and that surely had influenced the members of his household, including the ten children. However, it is not just that he was an abolitionist as an individual. It seems that his church, the Free Will Baptist Church, had adopted a strong position against slavery.

While we have no record of statements by the local Free Will Baptist Churches in Mayfield, Maine and in Adamsville, Pennsylvania, there is a record of the posture of the larger Free Will Baptist Church. In his book *"The War Against Proslavery Religion: Abolitionism and the Northern Churches, 1830-1865,"* John R. McKivigan states:

> *Evidence of the difficulties that abolitionists faced in dealing with the churches can be seen in their failure to obtain the unqualified support of even the small sects with long-standing antislavery traditions. The AASS (American Anti-Slavery Society) had few complaints regarding the Freewill Baptist's enthusiasm for abolitionism. A predominantly New England faith, the Freewill Baptist did not have a significant Southern consistency to placate in the slavery debate. Although their congregational policy made it impossible to establish a uniform rule barring slave-owning members, they found other ways to signal their opposition to slavery. The denomination's periodical, the Morning*

Star, began advocating immediate emancipation as early as 1834.
(McKivigan 43)

We know that Samuel's father-in-law, John Ellis, was an abolitionist, and that the members of his family belonged to a church that took a denominational stand against slavery. From this, we can infer that Silence would have made her strong feelings known to Samuel. We do not have Silence's letters to Samuel, but we can infer from his responses the religious concerns that she had during his absence.

Although Samuel made reference in many of his letters about his relationship to God, to prayer, to reading the Bible and other references to his faith, it is unclear how much of a practicing Christian he was before he entered the army. In this letter, quoted earlier, he said that he was not a practicing Christian:

May 4, 1865 Headquarters 9ᵗʰ Army Corps   Alexandria, Virginia #42

Silence, don't neglect to pray for me, for I know you are a Christian and how wicked I have been that I was not one, also, but if God spares my life, I shall be one, too. I feel happy all the time, but fear I am still in darkness.

However, in that same letter he said that if his life is spared, he would be committed to a Christian life when he returned home.

May it be the Lord's will that we may all safely return to our respective homes where we may forever worship Him, that is every watchful over us.

Although he said that he was not a Christian before entering the service, he was surely on a journey to become more of a Christian from the beginning of his time away from home in the service. From his letters, it certainly seems that his experience over the next nine months increased his faith. In his second letter, Samuel talked about his faith and his involvement in church. Might we infer that Silence armed him with a Bible before he left home, and that she was prodding him about his faith and church attendance during the nine months?

September 12, 1864   Camp Reynolds   #2

Silence, do not fret and feel sad about me, for I am able to take care of myself, only remember me in your prayers . . . . I was to church last night, which I intend to do as long as I am in the service of my country . . . . My God, I am sad, but God will take care of me.

He carried his Bible with him and made many references to reading it:

October 11, 1864   Bermuda Hundred Near Point of Rocks #7

Remember me in your prayers and I will do the same. Last Sunday we did not get rest. We had to clean our guns and then come out in dress parade. Then we had to stand picket duty at night. We have no Sundays here, but I do not forget my Book.

With the little family at home, in his prayers he constantly asked to be returned safely:

October 23, 1864   Bermuda Hundred   #9

If my health continues good I shall be a happy man and I thank my God every day. I hope He may spare my life to return home again to spend the balance of my days with my little family.

Each regiment had a chaplain and, in this case, Samuel was very pleased with him. In this letter, he made his first reference to his soul:

October 31, 1864   Camp Bermuda Hundred, Butler Headquarters#11

We also have an excellent chaplain with our regiment, from Venango County near Franklin, who preached yesterday at the Company headquarters outdoors. A very large audience were out in attendance. I could not help shedding tears to hear him preach to us poor soldiers. I feel happy, or in other words I feel as though nothing troubled me and perfectly contented with my lot as a soldier. My daily prayer is for God to have mercy upon me as a sinner. So do not concern yourself about the welfare of my soul, but don't forget me in your prayers, that

I may be spared and return home and live the balance of my days with you and my children—a Christian.

In the very early months of his service, one sees that he is promising to be committed to his family, and to being a Christian.

This letter shows his longing for home and his desire to become involved with his church:

November 23, 1864   Camp Bermuda Hundred   #14

I wish the war was over, for I long to get home to my family—if I am spared to go home, I shall live a different life, or a Christian life. I pray to my God every day that I must become a good Christian. I hope He may convert my soul to God. I am determined to serve my God. I feel better that I did when I left . . . . I hope I may return home again so you and I can go to church together. I mean to buy a horse and buggy, if possible. Remember me in your prayers and I will do the same with you . . . . I have a little book that I got from Christian Commission. It is a good little book.

Samuel was saddened by the sight of men being so ready to kill each other, and that moved him to a stronger position in his faith. He seemed to be struggling with what is involved in become more Christian:

December 1, 1864   Army of the Potomac Front of Petersburgh #16

I hope this war will soon come to a closing. Sometimes I feel sad to see men standing and watching their fellow men with the weapons of war and when the first opportunity affords itself, send him to Eternity with the content of your weapons. Oh what a solemn thought if that should be my fate. I sincerely want to be ready to meet my Maker.

You have asked me a serious question, in regards to my being converted or a child of God. I do not feel as though I have experienced religion, but I do feel as though I had an interest. I can say that I feel happy in my secret prayers to my God. I am determined to be a Christian. I hope you still pray for me at dinner. May God protect you in your sleeping hours.

There was time for reading the Bible and contemplation:

> *December 5, 1864   Headquarters Army of the Potomac   #17*
>
> *I lay around the shanty, read my Book, and write. The brass band is playing a mournful piece—how solemn it sounds. May God bring this Rebellion to a close and convert every soldier now in the field, for there are some awful wicked souls.*

Similar reflections a few days later:

> *December 18, 1864   Army of the Potomac, Virginia   #19*
>
> *Mr. Rodgers thinks there are some hard boys in our regiment. I think so myself. Roberts knows you very well. I presume you know him, don't you? I believe he is a good man, or a Christian. May God convert my soul. I am resolved to try and try until I experience religion and be on the right side of my Maker. I feel earnest in what I say. I pray the Lord may spare my life to get home to enjoy the happiness with my wife and children the balance of my days. May God be with you and your family.*

Every one of the men feel the pain of separation from their families.

> *January 1, 1865   Headquartered 9th Army Corps   #21*
>
> *I tell you it is good in old Virginia. It is now between 4 and 5 o'clock. The bugle horn starts blowing, the drums are a beating. The pickets are firing to keep the Jonnies from charging upon our lines. Now and then you can hear a cannon go chabung. The world here is full of commotion. Every man here knows his duty. It seems hard that men have to go stand for years in the cold and wet to watch the treacherous Rebels. I hope God will stop this terrible war. Let men return to their respective firesides with wife and dear children. I cannot help feel affected when I write, nor can I hear a man talk of such things but the tears come to my eyes. I do not know what is the reason, but that is the way I feel.*

In this letter, one sees insights into Samuel's soul. He expressed profound sadness, but could not articulate why he felt as he did.

Samuel began to read the Bible diligently:

January 15, 1865   Headquarters Army of the Potomac   #23

I am very well but cannot sleep all night. I am generally up in the morning about 4 o'clock reading my Testament. I have commenced to read straight through.

More questions from Silence about his ability to attend a church service:

January 24, 1865   Headquarters Army of the Potomac   #24

You wanted to know how I spend my Sundays, or at least the Sunday of the 15th. I spent it reading my Book—that I keep for my Guide. I love to read it more and more every day. Fret not about me. I will take care of myself, also of my Soul. I pray that God will see me safely home again to my beloved little family.

Here are several of Samuel's vows to be a strong Christian after he returns home:

February 1, 1865   Headquarters 9th Army Corps   #26

I thank you from the bottom of my heart for your kindness and trouble which I am constantly putting you through. I do not know whether I can ever repay you. I hope in the end to spend my days with you, a true Christian and a loving husband, and a Christian father. That is my full determination. I pray whenever I have the opportunity to my God to spare my life and spare me to go home again.

April 16, 1865 Burkville Station Headquarters 9th Army Corps   #38

Silence, I can't write much for I have no place to write, only on the ground. You can hear all the war news at home. Thank God the war is about to come to a close. That we men that have friends dear to us may be spared to return home to them where we may enjoy a Christian life with those that have been pious and said and done to persuade them to share an interest in the love of Christ. I still am determined

to be a Christian and pray to my God every day for the conversion of
my soul.

As the soldiers were preparing to go home from Alexandria and had no
real work to do, many turned into the rabble they were during the first
days of their enlistment:

The soldiers are all complaining and lying about. They say—why don't
the government discharge us and let us go home? Then they will curse
and swear and get drunk. There is nothing too bad for them to say or
do. They don't even thank their Heavenly Father for the preservation
of their wicked souls to the present time. No, they don't think the Lord
has any control over them. Oh, what a wicked people. It seems as
though they disregarded God and man. God is a merciful God, as one
have been in this war would have been cut down for their wickedness,
which they have committed in using profane language. I would not
dare to attempt the like. I think sometimes when I read God's word and
pray to him for forgiveness and thank Him for health and strength, I
fall short of doing my duty.

Is it possible that Samuel's journey of faith during his nine months'
service provided some protection of his soul? Although his soul was
wounded, did it survive in better shape because he was so involved in
his journey to a deeper commitment to Christianity?

Partly because of the experiences he had during his nine months
in the Union Army, and partly, I infer, from the diligence of Silence
and her religious life—and her questions, Samuel grew in his faith
during that time. He did return to an active church life in Crawford
County, Pennsylvania. By the time he entered the service, the Free
Will Baptist Church in Adamsville had dissolved, so they had changed
their membership to the church of Reverend H. H. Hervey, the United
Presbyterian Church of Hartstown. Note how many times Samuel refers
to his "soul."

From what I know personally, the children of Samuel and Silence, Myron
Manson Miller and Milo H. Miller, were active in churches throughout
their lives. As a boy of about eight years, I recall visiting the new building
of the Methodist Church of Hartstown, Pennsylvania. Grandfather

Myron Manson Miller introduced us to the new building with great pride. The previous church building had burned, and for a while the local Methodists were ready to travel off to Greenville, Pennsylvania and not bother trying to rebuild the local Methodist Church, but Grandfather would have none of that. Thus, he convinced the local Methodists to rebuild, and we saw the new building within days of its reopening in 1940. Milo H. Miller was a lifelong, active Presbyterian. Samuel and Silence were diligent in raising their two boys in the Christian church, and that commitment has passed down to this day.

Chapter 17

Epilogue

Prior to the Civil War, Samuel K. Miller had a shop near Hartstown, Pennsylvania. He was a cabinet maker and also tended his small acreage raising corn, beans, potatoes and garden vegetables. He was a good workman, so the little family had a relatively comfortable living.

In his book *A History and Genealogy of the Miller Family: 1725-1933,* Milo H. Miller wrote that the years following the Civil War were among the most prosperous that Hartstown had ever known. It was a period of inflation and rapid development. Oil had been discovered in northwestern Pennsylvania, and that furnished employment for thousands of men and affected the lives and fortunes of many others. Hartstown shared in that prosperity. The town was situated on the Beaver and Erie Canal at the foot of a reservoir that served as a feeder to the levels below. This large body of water became the favorite resort for the sportsmen of the surrounding country.

Hartstown is located in the midst of fine farming country. At that time, there were many stores and little shops where the local farmers could exchange the products produced on their farms for what they needed on a daily basis, like food and clothing. The town had a large saw mill, where the white pine timber, which was in abundance in that part of Crawford County, could be shaped into lumber and send to market, some rather distant from Hartstown. There was even a barrel factory at which quite a few men from the surrounding area worked. Those barrels were needed in the newly-prosperous oil fields of northwestern Pennsylvanian. Oil had been struck in Titusville, Pennsylvania in August 1859.

When Samuel returned from the Civil War in 1865, the Hartstown area was prospering, so his cabinet-making business also benefited immediately. It wasn't long until he needed a business partner to handle all the business he had. Samuel diversified his cabinet-making business into making coffins and then into undertaking. Initially, all the coffins were made in his shop, but as the business grew, he purchased coffins from Pittsburgh. When an order was received for a coffin, both Samuel and his partner, Charles Greenawalt, immediately started to work on it, and they would work straight through the night if necessary. By the next morning the coffin's woodwork was finished, at which point Silence did the trimming of the coffin, usually lining the coffin with white muslin. To make the coffin particularly attractive, she attached the muslin with gold or silver-headed nails. The final touch was the insertion of a pillow stuffed with cotton.

By eleven o'clock in the morning, the coffin was ready. Samuel conducted that business for many years and, in the process, became a very well-known citizen in the town. Ironically, Samuel's undertaking business benefited, sadly, from an epidemic of scarlet fever that killed hundreds of children in and around Hartstown. That epidemic coincided with a period of depression and general business failures from 1873 to 1878. Even though the nation was going through a very hard time because of that depression, Samuel's business did very well. (Miller, *Miller* 113)

After his years of building his cabinet-making business, then the undertaking business, he added a new dimension to his life's work. In 1878, he was appointed as the postmaster for Hartstown. Although he was fifty-six years old, he was still quite energetic. His appointment came about because there was a Republican President, and he had been a lifelong Republican. Also, because he was a well-known Civil War veteran and a leading citizen because of his role in local business, he was supported for that position by some of he leaders in Crawford County. With the help of Congressman Sam Dick and Captain Arthur J. Huidekoper, he was fortunate to get that assignment.

Samuel had served under Captain Huidekoper in the 211th Regiment; it had been Captain Huidekoper who had recommended Samuel for the Mounted Pioneer Corps! Now, in 1878, Captain Huidekoper had a significant role to play in the life and career of Samuel Miller, by helping Samuel become the postmaster in Hartstown. Sometimes we are fortunate to have "angels" in our lives who see our talents and our gifts, even better than we do. In that way, they lead us to opportunities that are often life-changing:

> [Rutherford] *Hayes was now the President of the United States. Father assumed the duties of the office in the spring of 1878 and served until the election of Cleveland in 1885—a period of seven years. In those days postmasters were appointed to office for services rendered to the party rather than upon merit as determined by a civil service examination.* (Miller, *Miller* 113)

Fortunately, all the letter boxes and the building were not dismantled in 1885 when Samuel ended his assignment, for in 1897, the postmaster position was back in the family. His son, Myron Manson Miller, became postmaster on July 15, 1897 and served until about 1942! The story is told that a post office official visited little Hartstown about 1941 (or so) and asked Myron why he was still working in his 80s. His response was 'Well, no one ever told me to quit!'"

When I was a young boy, the post office was still in operation and my grandfather was still the postmaster. The front part of the building, which was located on the corner of the family's property, was dedicated to the post office operation. My grandfather filled the hours, apart from his postmaster role, working at tanning and harness making in the back half of that building. Never an idle moment! I was fascinated by Grandfather's harness making equipment, and the wonderful smell of the place (not everyone would have agreed!). There was a pot-bellied stove in the center of the post office, so the men would gather about the warmth of that stove when they came to pick up the daily mail. The women in the neighborhood might pick up the mail rather quickly and stop by to see my grandmother in the kitchen before heading back home for their daily chores. My grandparents didn't lack for daily contact with their neighbors!

More from the pen of Milo H. Miller, Samuel's son:

> *Father continued to work at his trade for a number of years after the inauguration of Grover Cleveland and the removal of the post office to Findley's store. He repaired old furniture for his neighbors and friends*

and did odd jobs about the house and yard. He build a secretary and book case for me and managed to keep himself engaged until his health began to fail in the fall of 1895. He died of Bright's disease April 23, 1896 after a brief illness. He was not quite 74 years of age at that time. (Miller, *Miller Family* 114)

Samuel was survived by his widow and two sons, Myron and Milo, also by four grandchildren. As mentioned above, Myron was the postmaster in Hartstown for many years and a leading citizen in the community. Milo H. Miller became a leading educator in Western Pennsylvania. In 1890 he became the principal of the Walnut Street School in McKeesport, Pennsylvania. In 1899 he was appointed to the principalship of the Knoxville Public Schools, and became a leader in his church and the community. From what I have learned from his work in publishing genealogies of the Miller and Ellis families, and from his dairies which he kept from 1882 until 1940 and his other writings, Milo truly was a Renaissance man. It was he who kept Samuel's letters for many years, ultimately passing those on to a grandnephew, Kenneth Marcus Miller, who kept them for many years. At Kenneth's death, his widow Lydia Anna Miller, also kept the letters for many years before contributing them to the Crawford County Historical Society in Meadville, Pennsylvania.

A very nice tribute to Samuel Miller was included in the book, *History of Crawford County, Pennsylvania 1885*. That publication includes biographies of some of the leading citizens of the county at that time.

S.K. MILLER, postmaster, Hartstown, was born in Adams County, Penn., May 14, 1822, and is a son of John and Elizabeth (Shriver) Miller, natives of this State. His father was a blacksmith, and removed from this State to Ohio in 1823, settling near Petersburg, Ohio, and his family consisted of eleven children, of whom six survive, four now in Crawford County. These four are Jesse, Hiram P., Elizabeth (now Mrs. Mayo, near Atlantic), and S.K. Our subject now lives in this township [West Fallowfield] and was married January 29, 1857, to Silence, daughter of John Ellis. They have two children, Myron M. and Milo H., Mrs. Miller was the third in her father's family of ten children. Mr. Miller enlisted September 2, 1864 in the Two Hundred and Eleventh Pennsylvania Volunteer Infantry, and served during the balance of the war; he was appointed Postmaster August 6, 1878 and still holds that office, and makes an excellent official. Politically he is a Republican.

Samuel and Silence were members of the Free Will Baptist Church in Adamsville until the time of its disorganization, after which they transferred their membership to the U.P. (United Presbyterian) Church of Hartstown. Samuel died in 1896 and is buried at the Hartstown Cemetery, alongside his wife Silence, who died in 1899. (Bates II 1140)

And so ends the saga of Samuel K. Miller, who was drawn into the Civil War in 1864, served well and honorably until his discharge in June 1865. His experience as a Mounted Pioneer was rather unique, and helped him survive the Civil War. That role did not take away the loneliness of being away from his wife and two very young sons. That loneliness, combined with the horrors of war and the battles he experienced, had a strong effect on the strengthening of his Christian faith, and on his soul.

Appendix A

A Guide to Reading the Letters:
Who were the people, where were the places, what did he read?

To help make the reading of the letters more meaningful, I have attempted to describe the people to whom he referred in his letters. Where the people were family members, it is easier to identify them. When he refers to his fellow soldiers, we can often find them listed with his regiment or the other Pennsylvania units in the Civil War, although some do not appear in the final roster of the 211th Pennsylvania. Quite a few of those mentioned were friends or neighbors in—or nearby—his home town of Hartstown, Crawford County, Pennsylvania.

Both Samuel and Silence came from very large families, and Samuel either corresponded with them or mentioned them in his letters. Silence Ford Ellis came from a family of ten children; her parents were John and Susan Ann Ellis. There were nine children in Samuel's family, though one died very young; his parents were John and Elizabeth (Shriver) Miller.

Their families were:

The Ellis family, Silence's people

Enoch and Benjamin Ellis. When Samuel was stationed at Petersburg, Virginia, Enoch and Benjamin were serving in the 150th Regiment, Pennsylvania Volunteer Infantry. They were mustered into service August 30, 1862 at Harrisburg, Pennsylvania. That regiment was sent to Washington, DC and assigned to guard duty in and around the city. Company K, in which Enoch and Ben served, was stationed at the

Soldiers Home, the summer residence of the President. This company continued to act as the President's bodyguard until after the assassination of President Lincoln. The home was about three miles north of the White House. The buildings were stone and President Lincoln and his family occupied the mansion during the summer months, and returned to the White House during the colder months of the year. To keep guard, night and day, of this residence and the White House was the duty of Company K.

At one point, there was a move to transfer Company K to the front, where more men were needed after some battles had depleted the ranks of the 150th, but the President decided that so long as it was necessary for "any guard to remain, none would be more satisfactory than that of Captain Derickson and his company." Therefore, Company K stayed in that role until the end of their service June 15, 1865.

Mary, most likely Mary (Kinney) Ellis, wife of Benjamin. Benjamin Ford Ellis had been born in 1825, so he was 37 years old when he entered the service in 1862. His wife Mary Kinney Ellis, was born in 1826. When Benjamin entered the service, they had three children at home, ages 13, 11 and 7. She would have stayed home caring for the children during Ben's three years of service.

Samuel and his brother-in-law, Enoch Ellis, seemed to have had a very close relationship, because they shared many letters and visited each other somehow, Enoch in Washington and Samuel in or near Petersburg. In 1864, Enoch would have been 30 years old, and Benjamin 39 years old.

Kez, actually Keziah Hilcolm Ellis. In 1864, Keziah would have been 37 years old. She had been born in 1827 and married in 1846 to John Wright. They moved to Meringo, Iowa. He died in 1956, so Keziah moved with her children back to Hartstown, where she lived until 1894. One of her sons, Martin L. Wright was born in 1847 and, at a very young age, also joined Company K of the Pennsylvania 150th, so he joined his uncles in Washington, DC as a guard to the President. Another of Keziah's sons, Thomas McChesney, was in Company B of the Pennsylvania 76th Volunteers.

Ab, actually Abner Ford Ellis. In 1864, Abner was 34 years old, living in Hartstown. Abner was a farmer and very involved in the Methodist Episcopal Church of Hartstown. Abner had five sons and five daughters. Of those, five were born by 1864; their birth years were 1857, 1859, 1861, 1862 and 1863, so it isn't surprising that Abner did not serve in the Civil War, with such a large family.

Mag, probably Margaret (Rudy) Ellis, wife of Abner Ellis. Usually mentioned only as "Mag."

Nathan Ford Ellis, usually referred to as "Nate." Nathan was attending Hillsdale College in Michigan and was a senior when the Civil War broke out. He and his entire class left their studies and joined the Union Army on October 2, 1861. He was mustered out on August 17, 1863 and returned to Jackson, Michigan. Samuel would likely have had contact with this brother-in-law, since Nathan was back in the Hartstown area by the time that Samuel went into the service in 1864.

Philander Coburn Ellis, often referred to as "Cobe." Significant reference is made to Philander in this book, because he was killed at Gettysburg on July 2, 1863 in a famous charge by the First Minnesota. He had moved from Pennsylvania to the lumber regions of Minnesota to work, and was one of the first to enlist when Lincoln called for volunteers. He was mustered into the service as a private April 29, 1861 at Fort Snelling, Minnesota, to serve for three years. He was wounded in action at Bull Run July 21, 1861 and sent as a prisoner to Richmond, Virginia. After a time he was released and sent to Jefferson Barracks, near St. Louis, where he was paroled and went home on furlough. He returned to his command on December 22, 1862, in time to take part with his regiment in the battle of Gettysburg. He was killed in a desperate charge upon the Confederate lines on the evening of the second day of that battle, July 2, 1863.

From what we know of Samuel's travels after he left Petersburg, Ohio in earlier years, it seems likely that Samuel and Philander had worked and lived in proximity to each other for some period in Minnesota, prior to 1857 which, by that time, Samuel had returned to Pennsylvania and married in that year.

Alfreda Ellis. At the time of Samuel's service, Alfreda was 33 years old, married and living in Iowa. She had 10 children. As one of Silence's two sisters, it is very likely that Silence maintained frequent contact with Alfreda.

Lorenzo Dow Ellis, usually referred to as "Dow." Lorenzo Dow Ellis was named for a famous abolitionist in New England. He was the youngest in the family. He would have been 26 years old in 1864 when Samuel was serving. Dow married in 1863 and had a first child early in 1864. Eventually there were seven children in that family.

Cyrus Stilton Ellis, sometimes called "Tilt." Cyrus would have been 28 years old when Samuel was serving in 1864, and living in Kansas with his wife and first few of what were eventually eight children. There seems to have been relatively little contact between Cyrus and Samuel.

From the letters, one will see that there was frequent contact, directly or indirectly through Silence, with most of the Silence's Ellis families.

The Miller family, Samuel's people

Myron Manson Miller. My grandfather was born February 22, 1859, so he was five years old when Samuel entered the service. Myron was named after a famous Greek sculptor, who lived 480 to 440 BCE. Myron was one of the greatest sculptors of Early Classical Greek sculpture. He was famed for his sculptures of powerful athletes and life-life animals. He produced mainly bronze sculpture and was considered a versatile and innovative artist in his time. His most famous works, none of which have survived, include Discobolus, a discus thrower, and a bronze sculpture of a cow. The period when Myron lived has been called the "Golden Age of Athens," or "The Age of Pericles."

That Samuel and Silence would have named a son after a famous Greek sculptor indicates that one or the other, or both, had either studied Greek history in their schooling, or studied that period independently. It gets better!

Milo H. (born with the middle name Meade) Miller. Milo, my great uncle, was born in September 1863, so he was only one year old when his father entered the service. The name Milo also comes from ancient

Greece. The Milo of ancient Greece, Milo of Croton, lived near the same time as the sculptor Myron. Milo of Croton was a great athlete, primarily as a wrestler but also outstanding in all the sports of the time. It was said that as a little boy, he could hold a small animal above his head; when older he could hold a full grown, large animal over his head. He was also credited with being an important leader and victor in battles.

That Silence and Samuel would name both of their sons for the outstanding men of ancient Greece is additional evidence of their having studied and been very interested in ancient history, particularly that of Greece.

John Miller, Sr. Samuel's father was still alive during 1864 and most of 1865, living in Petersburg, Springfield Township, in what is now Mahoning County, Ohio. Samuel's father died December 4, 1865. Samuel doesn't mention his father in his letters.

Jacob Miller. Jacob was the second oldest son in the family, and would have been 58 years old in 1864. He was married in 1829 in Petersburg, Ohio, to Barbara Maurey. Like his father, Jacob Miller Sr., he learned the milling business and kept up the family trade to the end of his life. From a map in the late 1800s, it seems that he took over the mill and the property that his father occupied in 1823.

John Miller, son of Jacob Jr. John Miller, Jr., son of Jacob, was only eight years younger than his uncle, Samuel K. Miller. Although John was Samuel's nephew, because they were only eight years apart, it is likely that they were rather close because they lived in the same town, Petersburg, for almost 20 years.

John Miller, son of Jacob Sr. This older brother of Samuel would have been 54 years old in 1864 when Samuel was taken into the service. He moved to Michigan, where he eventually died in Sturgis, Michigan. It is not clear whether some of the references to John are to this John, his brother, who lived in Michigan or to the nephew John Miller who lived in Petersburg, Ohio. When Samuel makes reference to John Miller in Petersburg, then it is his nephew.

Jesse Miller. Jesse would have been 49 years old in 1864. Jesse was married in 1840 in Springfield Township, Ohio and then seemed to have lived there until 1875, when they moved to Hartstown, Pennsylvania. He owned a small grocery store in Hartstown.

Elizabeth Miller. Elizabeth married Loring Mayo of Warwick, Massachusetts on April 4, 1839 and they settled near the town of Atlantic, Crawford County, Pennsylvania. Elizabeth would have been 46 years old when Samuel was taken into the service. It seems that Elizabeth and her husband were the first of the Miller family to settle in Crawford County. After his several years in the upper Midwest, Samuel moved back east and moved in with the Mayo's in 1856. It was soon thereafter that he met Silence and married her in January 1857 in Adamsville, a nearby town. Whether it was Elizabeth who provided the attraction for her brothers from Ohio to Crawford County, we are not sure, but can speculate that as the one sister in the family, and apparently a very attractive and lively lady, the brothers would have found good reason to be in Crawford County near her.

George W. Donaghy. George Donaghy married Elizabeth (Miller) Mayo's oldest daughter Emaline Mayo on March 27, 1860. George would have been 30 years old in 1864 and Emaline 24 years old, so while significantly younger than Samuel, that couple could very well have been very close friends and relatives with Samuel and Silence. George Donaghy, originally from Butler, Pennsylvania ended his days at the old Mayo homestead. Emaline died at age 90; George at age 66.

Hiram Miller. Hiram Miller, the youngest of the nine children of John and Elizabeth (Shriver) Miller, would have been 37 years old when Samuel entered the service. He was surely the adventurer in the family. He was attracted to the Gold Rush in California in 1848, and in 1852 found his way to California by the way of Panama, where he crossed the Isthmus by mule train, and then by boat to California. Eventually he left California and returned to Pennsylvania, where he married in 1860 and settled into farming. Hiram married a Miss Emily Henry, the daughter of John Henry, who served in the Union Army with Samuel. Hiram was very active in the Grange and an elder in the United Presbyterian Church In Hartstown. He was also a member of the Independent Order of Odd Fellows, as later were other members of the family (including my grandfather Myron Manson Miller, who has the three circles of the Odd Fellows on his gravestone).

Unlike the Ellis family, which had four men in the Civil War in the Union Army, Samuel was the only one of that Miller family to serve. The brothers of Samuel were either too old, or had recently married and had one or more children by the beginning of the Civil War.

Some people who lived in Hartstown who were significant in Samuel's life were:

Mr. Benoni Ewing. Benona Ewing had the general store in Hartstown, and it was to Mr. Ewing that Samuel provided his military payments, upon which Silence drew for her family provisions.

Dr. White. We can infer that Dr. White was a physician but also seemed to be a person who Samuel trusted for advice on a variety of important personal matters.

Charles Carothers. Charles Carothers married Alfreda Ellis, Silence's sister. Alfreda and Charles were married May 5, 1855. Samuel mentions "Charley" and number of times, as well as "Charley's folks," and specifically Charles Carothers.

Mother. The mother mentioned quite often was Susan Ann (Ford) Ellis. Susan Ann's husband, John Ellis, had died during a trip that those two had made back to their previous home in Maine in October 1862. Therefore, when Samuel was in the service, Susan Ann had been widowed only two years, so it is very clear that Silence was very attentive to her recently widowed mother who lived nearby in Hartstown. Silence's mother died in 1869.

Mary Davis. During the time that Samuel was in the service 1864-1865, Silence took in Mary Davis as the housekeeper, helping to take care of the children and general housekeeping tasks.

Reverend H. H. Hervey, pastor of the United Presbyterian Church of Hartstown, Pennsylvania. After the dissolution of the Free Will Baptist Church in Adamsville, Samuel and Silence transferred their membership to the United Presbyterian Church of Hartstown. Reverend Hervey was Samuel's minister at the time when Samuel went into the service and in the end, assisted in Samuel's funeral.

The names of some of the citizens of Hartstown who are mentioned in Samuel's letters:

Quite a few people who lived in the Hartstown vicinity were mentioned in Samuel's letters. About most of them, little can be discerned, but about some he spoke not too kindly, implying that they were Copperheads.

- Mr. Manning—sold Silence a stove for $4
- David Russell—sometimes spelled Russle
- Joseph McQuiston
- Frank Hutchings
- George McGranahan
- Bill McLenahan
- Andrew J. Galbreath
- Plum Heagan
- James McHenry
- Bill Andrews
- John McGregor
- Ellen Johnson
- Robert McMichaels

I mention these people, because their descendants may find this book interesting. The mention of these people provides some insights into life in Hartstown during the Civil War period.

His fellow soldiers, either in Company A, in the Mounted Pioneers, or Pennsylvanians in other regiments of the 211th Pennsylvania. Those marked with an asterisk I have found in the roster for Company A:

- James Turner—from Meadville   *
- Robert Swartout—from Meadville
- I. S. Kean—from German's Corner
- Selkirk Wade   *
- Charles Swift—died Nov. 15, 1864   *
- Preacher Rodgers (probably John Rodgers)   *
- Frank (Franklin) Hutchins   *
- I.S. Kean
- Lieutenant Bates (Julius M)   *

- John Henry   *
- Mr. Blanchard (1st Sgt. D.WC. Blanchard)   *
- Jim Davidson
- Billy Trimble
- Bob McCaster
- Lyman Kilgore—probably Mounted Pioneer
- Thomas Gitcher—probably Mounted Pioneer

The descendants of these men could also find Samuel's story interesting, for they were in the Petersburg campaign with Samuel.

What was Samuel reading?

Like many other soldiers in the Civil War, Samuel was eager to get newspapers to get the larger picture of the war, as well as news from the home front. It seems that these newspapers were anti-slavery and/ or abolitionist, but that does not mean that that was the purpose for his reading those newspapers. As he stated early in his period of service, his primary purpose in volunteering was to save the union. In his letters, he shows sympathetic feelings toward the Negroes and slaves, but does not make statements that would indicated that he was abolitionist. It is clear from the letters and other family information that his wife and in-laws were abolitionist and would have been reading those newspapers in Crawford County during the early years of the war. Some of those he read were (to the extent I have been able to make inferences from his descriptions and information now available from other sources):

The Morning Star. It seems that this newspaper was published in Dover, New Hampshire. *www.seacoastnh.com/blackhistory/star.html.* According to the description in the site it was a radical anti-slavery newspaper produced by Free Will Baptists. There is no absolute certainty that this was the *Morning Star* that Samuel indicated he was reading, but by inference, there is a reasonable likelihood that this was the publication he read.

Since Samuel was associated with the Free Will Baptist, directly or indirectly, because his father-in-law and wife were Free Will Baptists from Maine, then later in Adamsville, Pennsylvania, one can infer that the family read that newspaper at their home in northwestern Pennsylvania.

It was originally published in Limerick, Maine then moved to Dover, New Hampshire in 1833. Although its anti-slavery stance almost ruined the paper financially for some time, it eventually prospered as people inside the Free Will denomination and many outside the denomination began to realize that slavery was an evil. The editor of the *Morning Star* stated at the annual conference in 1865 of the Free Will Baptist denomination that:

> *Since the last conference the Star has had the unspeakable joy of announcing the most important event of the nineteenth century, viz. The overthrow and, as we hope in God, the final death of American slavery, for which it has so long and arduously labored, and ardently hoped and prayed, but which at times it has almost despaired of living to see.*

It is likely that during the Civil War, Samuel read it because it was one that he had been reading at home, since marrying Silence in 1857.

The New York Tribune. Samuel made frequent reference to the *Tribune* which he endeavored to read whenever he could obtain one through the mail or in other ways. At the time of the Civil War, the New York *Tribune* was considered to have a radical Republican perspective. For the "radical Republicans," the only cause that justified going to war was the abolition of slavery. Chief among those newspapers: the *Tribunes* of New York and Chicago; and the Philadelphia *Inquirer.*

According to *Civil War Newspapers: A History Part I,*

> *The quintessential Radical paper was the New York Tribune, founded in 1841 by Horace Greeley, with the announced intention "to advance the interests of the people, and to promote their Moral, Political and Social well-being." Greeley promised that "the immoral and degrading Police Reports, Advertisements, and other matter which have been allowed to disgrace the columns of our Penny Papers [read: New York Herald] will be carefully excluded from this, and no exertion will be spared to render it worthy of the virtuous and refined, and a welcome visitant at the family fireside." Early on, the Tribune grabbed the abolitionist cause and never let go, earning the undying enmity of the Southern part of the nation.*

Further comments from this site *www.civil-war-newspapers.com* regarding the other politically oriented newspapers:

> *Moderate Republicans, who supported abolition but saw the struggle to preserve the Union: New York Times, Cincinnati Commercial, Boston Journal.*

> *Independents, against (or neutral on) abolition but which, for the most part, supported the government: New York Herald (although, to most Republican editors, the Herald was far from "Independent" and more likely "Democrat."*

> *Peace Democrats, Chicago Times.*

At one point, Samuel mentioned the *American Messenger* to Silence and sent her a copy. It was a monthly magazine, founded in 1842, featuring the writings of Christian preachers, writers and leaders who were popular with the public. It was published by the American Tract Society, a non-profit, evangelical organization,

Clearly, Samuel was reading the newspapers that were strongly anti-slavery and may also have been relatively informative when it came to coverage of the successes of the Union Army by the time Samuel entered the service in September 1864.

If he was sharing newspapers with the Confederates while on picket duty, as he claimed, he would most likely have read the Richmond *Dispatch,* the most important of the Southern newspapers. Other Richmond-based publications were the *Enquirer* and the *Examiner,* so Samuel may also have read those newspapers.

By 1860, there were 2,500 newspapers in the nation, of which at least 373 were published daily. Samuel usually seemed well informed about what was happening throughout the country related to the war, most likely because he had good access to the newspapers.

Appendix B

Letters of Samuel K. Miller:

The Petersburg Campaign 1864-65

September 9, 1864   **Camp Reynolds [Pennsylvania]**   **#1**

Most Affectionate companion & children,

Last night at 5 o'clock we were marched from the railroad which runs about 40 rods from this place. We arrived at Pittsburgh on the evening of the 5th about 9 o'clock at night, where we was put into a hog pen to put in the night. It was one of the filthiest places I ever saw in all my travels. There was great dissatisfaction amongst the boys but what could we do? There we were with a guard over us. But where we are now is the loveliest place you ever saw. The camp lays upon a high hill on the East side of the Monongahala River eleven miles above Pittsburgh.

We left Meadville on Monday at 10 A.M. for Ravenna, Ohio. There we changed cars for Wellsville and Pittsburgh, thence to our present destination. Our captain has not come yet but expect him today. There are about 5,000 boys here with their blues on. There are about 800 tents up. The soldier boys are most all married men, some 50 & 55 years old. But the majority are middle-aged men that have done as I have done—left their homes, some with wives only, and the rest with wives and from one to four or five little ones that are dear to them as mine is to me.

I am in good spirits and am not sorry that I have volunteered for my country. I am well, and have many merry times. Last night I heard praying and swearing, dancing and fiddling and singing. As for my part, I did neither. I bought myself a Testament to instruct myself when a soldier boy.

Selkirk Wade is in our company. Him and John Koury and Frank Hutchings and myself will tent together. We cannot tell how long we will be here, probably two weeks. Our company is not organized yet, therefore I cannot tell you where to or what company or regiment to direct.

Silence, I hope you are reconciled by this time. Keep in good spirits and try and get along the best you can until I return again, which I will certainly do. Don't starve yourself and children and go respectable in society. Your money lays at your command. Use what you want. I did not see Plum Hagen, but get it and use it for debts, etc. Give my respects to all that may inquire for me, especially my sister that I am sorry that she has treated me the way that she has. Silence; remember me in your prayers. Be kind to Myron and Milo. Myron, be a good boy and eat all the melons you can. Some day I will send you something pretty.

Goodbye for the present. I shall write again just as soon as our company is organized. That may be done today. No more from your affectionate husband.

Please do not show this to any one.

Samuel K. Miller

September 12, 1864   Camp Reynolds [Pennsylvania]   #2

We have just come in from drill, which gives us about two hours rest before dinner, so I thought my chance was good for writing. I am well and ready for my rations. I sincerely hope and pray that you and the children have good health. Silence, do not fret and feel sad about me, for I am able to take care of myself, only remember me in your prayers. I think a great many times about you and the little ones, but may God bless you and family and take care and watch over you.

I have not been any lonesome yet. I was to church last night, which I intend to do as long as I am in the service of my country. There is now in camp about thirteen thousand soldiers. At one o'clock today one regiment leaves for Washington. I just spoke to our Lieutenant Huidekoper how long we might remain here, but [he] could not give me a definite answer, but told me to write anyhow. Also said that you could write as soon as you received this, so I hope you will answer this immediately if it is not more than 10 lines, for I do want to hear from home so bad—how you get along—and who stays with you at night—and whether Liza has been up yet—and whether you can't get her to stay with you until I come back—if you have to pay her to stay. Have Reg and Mother come home yet and had she good health? A great many questions that I cannot think of, for there is so much confusion that I cannot think of much. I am writing on a portfolio that I bought at the city. We draw our government bounty here some day this week, which I will send home by express, but will write you when I send it.

That paper you got at the commissioners, take it to Esys Henry or Gordon and have it filled out so you can draw your relief money. I never went to the barracks at Meadville until Monday morning. If I had known that I might just as well stay at home with you. Parting is no harder one time than another. My God, but I felt sad, but God will take care of me.

Mr. Blanchard tents in our next tent. Selkirk Wade that used to live at Adamsville is in our company. John Kean is with us. He is from the neighborhood of Greenawatts. We have the best-hearted lot of men in our company that I ever saw. So clever and sociable—and a great many professors. No swearing and cursing like there is in most of the companies. I have heard more wickedness since I came to camp than I ever heard in all my life and travels.

I saw Hiram when at Nelson's station. Said he—Do you not hate to go? No—said I—am going to fight for my country. I have not written to him yet. I have not [written] to Jacob or John, but I will before a great while. Has there yet a draft made? If there has, let me know who was drafted from our township & county. All the news you can think of. Silence, I must stop writing and go my dinner. We draw our rations cooked, but it is very dirty, but we will soon cook our own grub.

Give my love to all that inquire about me. May God bless your soul abundantly. That is my feeling. Kiss Myron and Milo for me. Myron, be a good boy. Be kind to your Mother and your Brother Milo. So, goodbye for this time. I will write again. Your very affectionate
Direct to Camp Reynolds, Allegheny County, Pa., care of Capt. E. B. Lee

Write immediately.

Samuel K. Miller

September 17, 1864   Camp Reynolds [Pennsylvania]   #3

Dear Wife,

I received your letter today. Oh! but I was glad to hear from you and our little ones. How I long to see you but there is no use of talking about that yet. I am glad that you feel composed as well as you are. I am well and still in good spirits.

This evening at 4 o'clock we start for City Point, Virginia. What we will do then we are not able to tell, but I suppose will drill a while, then perhaps put into battle, but cannot tell anything about yet. I doubt our officers would be so cruel as that put us in front before we are thoroughly drilled. We also draw our guns here. There are ten companies in our regiment. The number of our regiment is 211 Pennsylvania Volunteer Company A, but will give you the proper directions when I write again and [it] will not be until we get to City Point, then we will know all about how to tell how to direct your letters.

You spoke about them bedsteads. If you wish, they may go. Let them have them at $5 each, then they can get them finished where they please.

There are a great many in camp that have the dysentery. I had a slight touch, but I am all right now. The reason why they have it so much is because they eat so much trash.

We left on Saturday night. We are now in Washington, Tuesday morning, 10 o'clock. I would like to see the boys [Benjamin and Enoch, his brothers-in-law] but cannot get a pass yet. If we stay here any time I shall go and see them. As I was going to say, we left Camp Reynolds Saturday evening at dusk, traveled all night and the next day to noon before we reached Harrisburg. Did not stop. Next place of importance was Little York. There we were saluted by the inhabitants with anxiety and welcomeness. We had what we could eat and twice as much as we could possibly consume. We gave them a hearty salute and away the iron horse rolled us onward. There were thirty-two cars loaded with dixey [Dixie] boys. Thence for Baltimore which arrived at midnight, where we were marched to the depot and there we took a good sleep on the floor. I stand it first rate. At one o'clock we started for Washington, which we arrived at 5 o'clock the same day, which was Monday.

This forenoon we was up to see the Capitol, which is the most perfect structure I ever saw, but no tongue can describe it. I would give fifty dollars if you were here to see it. It is all built of white marble, that is, the outside. The inside is all colors of marble. It is all marble, even the floors, steps. There is no wood about it all.

There is so much confusion that I cannot scarcely write but I will do the best I can. We got our government bounty pay, that is, $133.33. I will send you in this letter ten dollars, and the next letter I write I will send ten dollars more and so on until I get it all home. I bought me a pair of boots, which cost me nine dollars in Baltimore, and sold my shoes for $1.50, so my boots stands me $7.50. Silence, get the boys or some lady to get you winter wood. The weather is beautiful indeed, the roads are dusty, the sun very warm and pleasant. We have nice quarters and good grub, that is, coffee and bread and pork. Send me when an opportunity the Morning Star [a newspaper].

Silence, you may do with this money I send you what you please—dress yourself and children, and make yourself comfortable as you can. Take care of things as well as you can until I come home again. Get the cave fixed if you can. That is all I can think of. May God take care of you and watch over you when in slumber. Kiss my boys for me. I shall write again soon. Answer this soon. From your affectionate companion,

Samuel K. Miller

Direct Washington, D.C.

Company A, 211 Regiment P.V. care of Captain E. B. Lee or elsewhere

September 26, 1864   Camp of the 211 Pa.V. [Virginia]   #4

Only friend on earth,

I take the earliest opportunity to write again. I wrote you last at
Washington and now we are camped in Virginia, about two miles in the
rear of Bermuda Hundred, or in other words, two miles from the James
River, where Butler made the Rebels skiddadel last May. Butler's whole
force lays in sight of our camp. We all saw the old general last Saturday
evening passing by. He is a good-looking man and a brave man, I think
from his appearance.

We left Camp Reynolds last Saturday evening a week ago and arrived
this place Thursday evening dusk. We lay on the ground the first night.
Next day we all went to work and built pens 6 by 12 feet, about three
feet high, out of poles, then covered it with our tent cloths which makes
it very comfortable. We cannot tell how long we may remain here. We
can hear cannons fire all day and all night. We are just 10 miles from
Petersburg and 20 miles from Richmond.

The Rebels keep up constant fire at the canal where Grant is cutting. On
Saturday morning there were 100 guns fired in honor of the great victory
that Sheridan gained. The Newhire [?] reports a loss to the Rebels—5
thousand and five hundred killed, wounded and prisoners. The general
opinion is amongst old soldiers and citizens that Rebeldom cannot last
long.

I was up to the Soldier Home to Enoch [Enoch Ellis, his brother-in-law,
who was in Company K of the 150th Pennsylvania, which served as
bodyguards for President Lincoln] and Mart Wright [Martin Wright,
Samuel's nephew, daughter of Keziah Ellis Wright]. I never saw Mart
look any better in my life. He looks like a man and keeps himself clean

and trim. Enoch said that the time they were called out, Mart was the best soldier they had in the [regiment]. They have a fine place to stay and good times. I also was up to the President House but he was not out of his bed. I saw all the boys, etc.

When I wrote you last I sent you ten dollars. Let me know whether you received it or not. When my letters run through directly, I shall [send] 15 [dollars] more. Write all particulars and how you get along. I wrote to Jacob a few weeks ago. I gave it to him pretty hard. Let me know what the folks think about me volunteering. Hiram told me that Mayo thought I done right, but Eliza thought it awful. Let me know all about the draft, who was drafted.

I only received one letter since I left home, but am perfectly satisfied with one. I suppose there are more on the road for me. Write whenever you feel like doing so. I am middling well. I took a bad cold and it has made me very sore through the small of my back. I do not think that I can stand much backing, but I will do the best I can and that is all that anyone can do. Let me know whether Mother and Kez [Keziah, Silence's sister] has come home yet. Give my respects to Abner and Tilt [Cyrus Stilton Ellis, Silence's brother] and the boys to Doctor White's folks. Have you made your dress yet that I bought at Meadville? Pay my debts as they call on you. Write soon all particulars. Kiss the little boys for me. I hope you are well and enjoying yourself first rate. Get along as well as you can and take care of the property the best you can and may we all be home by next spring.

When you write Direct Samuel K. Miller, Company A, 211 Regiment, Pa.V. care of Capt. E. B. Lee. [He was killed on April 2, 1865 at the advance on Petersburg].

Washington, D.C.

October 3, 1864   Bermuda Hundred [Virginia]   #5

We are now in front of the Rebels, about on line between the two places which our armies [are] contending for—that [is] Petersburg and Richmond. Our army is fighting on our right and left, which we can hear very distinctly from where we lay. We are laying in the strongest fortifications, the old soldiers say, that is, except Grant's, where his army lays or is fortified. The Rebels have a fortification right on our front, probably 3/4 of a mile. Our picket lines lay between these two fortifications where we and the Rebels have to stand picket.

The first night I was out, there was 6 Rebels came to our lines. Oh, but they were glad when they got to us! They said there was twenty-seven in one company that said wanted to come to our lines. The weather here is warm and pleasant until a day or two [ago]. It has rained some this morning. About daylight we were routed out of our tents in a hurry to the Breast Works [trenches or chest-high structures intended to help protect the soldiers from enemy fire]. The alarm was that the Rebels was going to make a charge, but they failed to come. Our Batbies ([batteries?] gave them about fifty shots but they never returned the compliment. So we went back to camp probably 50 yards. I expect tonight I will be on picket. We have a great many that is considerable cowards. I am going to do my duty. I think the thing is coming to a close as fast as can be done. We could see them fight over on Malvern Hill across the James River, a distance of 5 or 6 miles. We could see the dust and smoke and shells bursting in the air.

I shan't write much this time only that I [am] still in good health and spirits. I have not received but one letter from you yet. But there are lots in our company that have not had any at all. I [hope] you and the children are well and getting along well. Don't forget those apple trees the 31 of this month and have them set out right, and keep the cow off of the lot. Silence, tell Ab to write to me. I would write to him but I have not had time since we came here to write anyone but you. My love to Mother and the boys and tell Tilt [Cyrus Stilton Ellis] to write Nate [Nathan Ellis, his brother-in-law] and Dow [Lorenzo Dow Ellis, another brother-in-law]. I will close hoping this may find you well. No more for now from your very affectionate husband. Write soon.

Samuel K. Miller

Direct Company A, 211 Pa. V. care of Captain E.B. Lee

Washington, D.C.

October 9, 1864   **Bermuda Hundred,**
                             Camp Near Point of Rocks [Virginia]   #6

Dear Brother [his brother-in-law, Enoch Ellis, stationed with the 150th Pennsylvania in Washington],

According to promise I take the first opportunity of writing a few lines to you. Since we came here we have moved most every day since we left the boat. We lay almost in line of Petersburg and Richmond. We can see Richmond very plain in a clear day. There has been some desperate fighting within the last week between the Yanks and Jonnies in sight of our fortifications towards Richmond. Our boys took two lines of fortifications with about 5,000 prisoners. The Rebs, not being satisfied, made 3 charges in one day but was repulsed every time with heavy loss each time. On the 6th the Rebs made one charge after another but whipped every time with very heavy loss. Our boys mostly have seven shooters [capable of shooting seven shots without reloading] and the Rebs say the Yanks shoot all the time and never load. They can't contrive what it means.

Our boys are now within four miles of Richmond. The [word] came in yesterday that the Rebs were evacuating Richmond and were going to Danville to concentrate there, but there are so many reports come every day that you cannot tell what is truth or what is not. The first night we stood picket we took in 7 Rebs into our lines. There were 5 that came in on my post. I tell you they were glad when they got into our lines. They were poorly clad and it rained all night and cold. They were very near froze.

Enoch, I shan't write very much for it is very cold and my hands are numb. I have only received one letter since I left home, that was at Camp Reynolds. I presume you hear from home often. Do you know whether Silence or any of the children are sick? If they [are], let me know. Enoch, what course must a man pursue in order to get a vote, or will there be provisions made by our Township officers so we do not lose our votes? If you know anything about it let me know immediately. Enoch, send me by return letter one dollar worth of postage stamps. I tryed to get some at Washington but could not get them Perhaps they can be had now if you can send them and I will send you the dollar by return mail.

I have had very good health with the exception 4 or 5 days but am quite well now. We have to stand picket duty every other night. I like it middling well. The first day we were here we were marched to the breastworks to make a demonstration. We had scarcely started up before we received a shot from the Rebs, but as luck would have it, the ball did not explode but killed two men in Company F next to Company A. I tell you we skiddaled down very quick. The Rebs fortifications lay about one mile in front of our fortifications. At one place our pickets are within one rod of each other. But they are civil and say they will not shoot unless we do. We are not permitted to speak to them nor trade with them, but they will trade coffee for tobacco and exchange papers, also.

Enoch, answer this just as soon as you receive this. Give my respects to Ben [Ben Ellis, his other brother-in-law, also with the 150th Pennsylvania stationed in Washington] and all the boys in your tent, etc. No more. Excuse bad writing. I wrote this on my knee. Yours with respects.

Samuel K. Miller

Direct S. K. Miller, Company A, 211 Regt. P. V. care of Captain E. B. Lee

Washington, D.C.

October 11, 1864   Bermuda Hundred Near Point of Rocks   #7
                        [Virginia]

Dear wife,

I received your letter last night and was very glad to hear from you that you were enjoying good health. The letter I read last night is the second one I got from you since I left home. I write to you every week—the last letter I sent you I sent another 10 dollars green back. I am well and hearty and in good heart. Today we vote for state officers. We had all our tickets sent us. Our regiment will most all go for the Republican ticket.

I must tell you that when we started for this place we marched through the city of Washington. There were two flags hanging across the street.

The first one was a McClellan flag. When we came about to it, we sallied off to the left of it, and we all commenced groaning and hissing. Then we came to old Lincoln. We marched right through under it and all cheered it very heartily. I tell you what a cheering there was for about half hour! I never in my life—by the citizens as well as by the soldier boys.

Silence, I want you to get me a pair of gloves, sheepskin or buckskin. Don't get very costly ones, and send them to me by mail. We cannot get them here for less than three dollars per pair—I think you can get them there for about $1.50. I want you when you write again let me know what kind of weather you have in Pennsylvania and what you can get corn for per bushel and how the hogs do and whether you have made the cave yet and whether you have dug the potatoes yet and if they rotted any.

The war is about played out. The Jonnies are coming into our lines every day. The Georgians have thrown down their arms and declare they will not fight any more. Grant has given them the permission of crossing our lines if the Rebels refuse them crossing their own lines. We have to stand picket about every other night. We can see the Rebs and talk to them and exchange newspapers with them—also trade coffee for their tobacco. They are awful afraid of us. They tell us when they are ordered to fire upon us they say they will shoot over our heads and they want us to do the same. They say if Lincoln is reelected that they are all gone up.

I wish you had sent for this Certificate a few days sooner. I am afraid you will not get this in time to do you any [good]. I would have sent you one long before now but they told me I did not need anything of the kind—that you could draw your money without [it]. I should of got this at Provost's Office at Meadville. But there was so much said concerning it that we did not know what to do, but I got one from our Captain this morning, if it is good for anything. Why, alright, and if not why, I do not know how to work it. I suppose you got my clothes that I sent home from Meadville. I sent them by Cleve Wade.

Ask Doctor White how we are to get our tickets for the Presidential election, whether they will be sent to us or not, or whether we will vote here. Tell him to give you some information about it.

The weather is most beautiful. The nights are rather cold but the days are very warm and pleasant. I think more than likely we will stay here this winter to do picket duty. There are now at Washington one hundred thousand soldiers waiting for transportation to the front. The canal is about finished at Dutch Gap. We can see it from camp. The Rebs are shelling our men that are to work at the canal every day. They are at it this morning, but the Rebs gets two shells back for every one the Rebs sends. I don't mind their shelling any more, for you can hear them and they fight almost every day in some direction.

Don't be uneasy about me. I am alright and feel reconciled about the future. Give my respects to all that inquire about me. Kiss Myron and Milo for me. I shall write every week to you. Keep in good spirits and do not fret about me for I am able to take care of myself. Remember me in your prayers and I will do the same. Last Sunday we did not get rest. We had to clean our guns and then come out on dress parade. Then we had to stand picket at night. We have no Sundays here but I do not forget my Book every opportunity. I shan't write any more at this time. There are 4 or 5 letters on the road for you. No more from me for the present. From your husband that respects you above any on earth—So good bye for the present.

Tell Myron there is another greenback coming for him.

Samuel K. Miller

October 17, 1864   Bermuda Hundred [Virginia]   #8

Dear Wife,

I received your letter—dated the 9th and mailed the 11th—today about half past nine o'clock. I was very glad, very indeed, to hear from you and family again. This is the third letter I received from you since I left home, and this one that I am now writing makes 7 or 8 that I have written to you. You stated that Mother and Kez have returned home safely again. I was very much pleased to hear of their safe arrival home. I hope Mother will be contented now. I am very glad that you have someone to stay with you, for company. Try and keep her all winter if you can. Perhaps you can persuade your Mother to stay with you. Have you ever heard from Liza Miller whether they want to come and stay awhile? Try and get along the best you can and I shan't find no fault.

You said in your letter that the folks blamed you for letting me come to war. Just tell them if they say anything to you again for me that I wished them to attend to their own business and let you alone while I am here in the service of my country. Tell them to wait until I come home and I will talk to them myself, and just say to Mag for me to keep her mouth shut and keep her guts warm. Tell them not to blame you for anything that I have done. Do not concern yourself about me. I am well and hearty, more so than I have [been] for six months. I was sick a few days but was not confined to bed at all. I got two doses of pills from John S. Kean and took them and they straightened me up. The worst trouble is with me now I can scarcely get enough to eat. We get hard tack and pork and beef and coffee and sugar, etc.

Tell them folks that told you that we was in a battle—tell them that is not the case. I think I can tell you what they are after, but I did not intend to tell you anything about [it] until after I got home. The second day after we got here we were marched to the breast works and were ordered to get upon them, that is, the whole regiment. We had not been there more than 10 minutes until the Rebs shot a shell at us passing through Company F, the next company to ours. It is the first in the regiment, then Company G, etc. The shell, as I said before, passed through F, killed one instantly and wounded one so bad that he died the same day. That was all the battle we were in—so you can tell how just how it was.

Frank Hutchins is in the hospital very sick. Mr. Blanchard has been sick with the fever for three weeks but is getting better. I could tell you a great many things but I have not time. I am detailed for picket tonight. I wrote you a letter some four days ago. I would like to have you send me a pair of sheepskin gloves lined with cotton flannel and send them by mail. I wrote a letter to Hiram a few days ago, also one to Enoch. Tell the boys to write to me for they have more time than I have. We have no Sundays here. Take care of yourself and I will do the same. I shall write to you again. Write often and I will do the same. Give my respects to all that inquire about me. No more, but from your husband, so good afternoon.

Direct as usual.

Tell Myron I will bring him lots of presents when I come home. I want you to be a good

[boy]—mind your mother.

Samuel K. Miller

October 23, 1864   Bermuda Hundred [Virginia]   #9

Dear Silence,

I cannot help writing to you when an opportunity affords itself. We just came in from dress parade. We [have] just as much to do on the Sabbath day as on week days. This evening we go out on picket duty and remain there 24 hours, then we are relieved by others. It requires 600 men to guard the line which is perhaps 3 miles in length. It is easy duty. We stand 2 hours on and 2 hours off, and day time 1 hour on and 4 off, etc. So goes the duties of war.

Silence, I am very well. I believe I never was heartier in my [life]. The boys all say I am getting as fat as a pig. I believe I never told you who my tent mates are. I will tell you. Selkirk Wade, I.S. Kean from Germans Corners—a first rate pious man, and James Turner from Meadville and Robert Swartout from Meadville and John Henry and myself. F. Hutchins is very sick. He is not expected to live. Our Lieutenant Bates was down to see him yesterday and he is bad.

If my health continues good I shall be a happy man and I thank my God every day. I hope He may spare my life to return home again to spend the balance of my days with my little family. Silence, I sent you a newspaper a few days ago called the American Messenger. I think you will like it. I also sent one to Mrs. Mayo. I done it merely to affect her feelings toward you and myself. May God bless her soul abundantly. I wish you would send me the Star [The Morning Star] or Tribune [New York Tribune] once in a while. It only costs two cents postage.

I got a letter from Enoch a few days ago. He stated that Ben was home sick. I wrote to Enoch to send me one dollar's worth of postage stamps, which he did. You spoke about how I liked woolen shirts. I like them very well. We have very good clothes, and warm. We drew our overcoats last week and gum blankets [a black rubber coated canvas, issued to each soldier]. They are nice on cool nights on pickets. We also get plenty to eat. Silence, when we pitch our winter quarters I want you to send me some apple butter and butter with Henry's folks. Butter is 80 cents per pound, sweet potatoes are 10 cents per pound, canned peaches $1.00 per can, onions 15 cents per pound, cheese 50 cents per pound and everything in proportion. We draw potatoes, beets, turnips, codfish, mackeral, fresh beef, salt beef and salt pork, coffee, sugar, bread and crackers, etc.

I think likely we will draw our pay by the first of next month

There is big excitement among the soldiers—the coming election. Old Abe is, I think, our president for four years more. The opinion is all through the army that this terrible Rebellion will close by spring or sooner. I suppose you have heard that Sheridan had one of the greatest victories a few days ago since the war commenced. He captured 47 cannons, all there ambulances, trains, and baggage train—with many prisoners—and killing and wounding, which we have not heard of yet.

Our batteries with 40 guns opened and fired 100 shots into the Rebel's fortifications perhaps a mile distant, killing five men in one tent and how many more we did not learn, so said a Rebel deserter which came into our lines that night, but the Rebs never replied one shot. They were, I presume, afraid. Silence, I will tell you all about [this] when I come home.

We have as pretty weather here as you ever saw in your life. The roads are dry and dusty as in midsummer, the sun shines clear and warm, but the nights are rather chilly. There has only been one or two frosts yet. The oak leaves are green as ever. Oh, what a desolate country! You cannot see a house, only now and then an old wood colored thing, but across the James River you can see probably ten or a dozen, where our army has not been, but I think the day is not far distant when there will not be the mark of a house.

The army on our left are on the move for Richmond, which will eventually tell what or whether we fight much more or not.

That certificate that I sent you will not do. Take our marriage certificate and go to Dr. Derickson at Meadville. Tell him you want a certificate. And [if] he does not believe you—that you are not my wife, just hand him that Book, etc.

My sheet is about filled. I am sleepy, so I will close hoping sincerely you and little ones are well, and try to do the best you can. Give my love to Mother and boys and Kez and tell the boys to write if they please. Don't work too hard and take care of yourself. I send Myron a cent. I would like to see the little fellows. Do not write any discouraging news, etc. Keep in good spirits and I will do the same. Write often, don't wait on me. From your very affectionate husband.

Direct as usual. I can read your writing, every word.

Samuel K. Miller

October 27, 1864   Bermuda Hundred [Virginia]   #10

My dear wife,

I received your letter dated the 18th of this month and was also very much pleased to hear from you again. I just sent you a letter a few days before receiving yours. I also received one from Abner in the same mail. Oh, but I was glad to hear that you were well, also the little ones. I am very well indeed. I have not had the headache since I came to Virginia—

Silence, I want you to go to town and buy a box of Wrights Indian Vegetable pills and send them to me by mail. Just as soon as you receive this. We have a great deal of sickness in our regiment. There are about 25 in our company that [have] the fever and ague [chills and sweating]. Mr. Blanchard is getting well fast, he is, so he can walk around the camp and do light work etc. Frank Hutchins is on the turn for the better with good care, and that he has, for he has a woman for a nurse. He is in the Sanitary Commission hospital. Silence, if you every have an opportunity of giving anything to the Sanitary [Commission] I want you to do so, for I think it is one of the finest institutions that is in our army for the poor sick and wounded soldiers.

You wanted to know if we had anything to do on Sunday. Yes, every Sunday morning we have our streets to police, that is, to clean them—then we [have] a dress parade, then a company inspection, etc. and then go to church if you choose. I heard through John Henry that Kez [Keziah, Silence's sister] was married to someone from Maine. Abner wants to borrow fifty dollars from me until spring. I think Ab is a pretty fine fellow and guess you may let him have it. Make him give his note and get all the interest you can.

I am now on the detail duty chopping timber for hospitals, so if there is any fighting to be done I shan't be into it. We are about six miles from camp. I think it will take about three weeks. The work is very easy.

There is one of the hottest battles commenced that has been since the war commenced. Yesterday about 11 o'clock they began fighting, continued until 1 this morning. We have not heard whether our boys were victorious or not but the sound of the cannon went almost out of hearing. Oh, what a terrible war this is. May God bring it to a speedy close that we may all return home.

Silence, I cannot write much this time for there is so much confusion, that I shall come to a close hoping you and family are enjoying good health and I pray that God may take care of you and the children. Do not forget me in your prayers. I have considerable but will write more in my next—. Write often and I will do the same. I am well and in fine spirits and I want you to keep in good spirits. I hope this may find you in good health. Good morning, I must go and get my breakfast and go to work. Excuse my short letter. Goodbye.

From your husband,

Samuel K. Miller

October 31, 1864   Camp Bermuda Hundred
Butler Headquarters   #11

Never forgotten companion,

I received your letter dated October 23rd last Friday evening the 28th. You may be assured that I was glad to hear from you and family. I also received one from Abner. The last letter I got from you was the fourth one I received since I came to the army, this one makes 9 or 10 I have written to you. This makes three that I have wrote in 10 days, but what do I care for a little time and paper, etc. I love to write to you. Yesterday I wrote to Brother John in Michigan.

When I think of it, Charles Swift is in our company, Mrs. Jacob Brown's brother. He requested me to say to you, for you to tell Mrs. Brown the first opportunity that he is sick and has been for eight days but is getting better and he would write to her in a few days if he continued getting better. [Charles Swift did not recover and died November 15, 1864].

I believe I never told you who all belonged to Company A that I was acquainted with—Isaac Graff, Osker Lee from the Lake, Jerry Millen Heandy from where Greenawalt. lives. I. P. Kean from Shermans Corners and Preacher Rogers that used to preach at Adamsville. Old drunken Bill Brown's oldest boy is in Company A. Mr. Rogers and a man by the name of Thurston were chosen or detailed when we first came here to guard an ammunition train, so you perceive he is not with us—but was up this morning to get his news and he gave me a Morning Star. I tell you I gave it a good perusal. It done me more good [than] if I had eaten my dinner.

We also have an excellent chaplain in our regiment from Venango County near Franklin, that preached yesterday at the Company headquarters outdoors. A very large audience were out in attendance. I could not help shedding tears to hear him preach to us poor soldiers. I feel happy, or in other words I feel as though nothing troubled me and perfectly contented with my lot as a soldier. My daily prayer is for God to have mercy upon me as a sinner. So do not concern yourself about the welfare of my soul, but don't forget me in your prayers, that I may be spared and return home and live the balance of my days with you and my children—a Christian.

The first opportunity I have I shall have my likeness [portrait] taken. I have shaved since I am out. I look pretty hard, but I feel well and hearty. I thank God for it. I am getting fat.

I wrote to you once before that myself and I.P. Kean were detailed to cut timber for hospitals, which will probably take us 3 weeks. There are about 200 men to work, which keeps us from the battlefield, if there should be any battles. Our colonel talks some of taking us to Washington to guard forts. There are nearly a fourth of our regiment sick with the ague. I hope he will succeed in accomplishing it. We are not well enough drilled for this place. We can see the bomb shells fly at night and burst as plain as the fingers on your hands but are not nearer than 1 1/2 miles from camp.

Tell Ab and Nate the canal is finished, all but the blowing out the ends. The Rebs throw shells into the canal every day and every night, but our men have bomb proofs made so they can run into when shot at. We expect a big battle in a few days. Last Thursday and Thursday night there was an awful battle near Petersburg. We could hear the cannonading just as plain as though they were not more than 1 mile off—but was some three miles distant. The skies were as light—I was going to say, as day. We have not yet heard the result of the battle.

I cannot think of anything more of interest to you, so I will close, hoping you and children are all well, also hoping to hear from you soon again. Give my respects to all that may inquire about me and be sure to take a good share yourself. Give my love to Mother. I am well and hearty. Myron and Milo be good boys until I come home and I will fetch you nice presents when I come. Be a good boy to Mother. I wrote this upon my knee, so excuse bad writing. Direct as usual. Your very affectionate husband,

Samuel K. Miller

**November 7, 1864   Butlers Headquarters,
Eight Miles in rear of
Bermuda Hundred   #12**

This is Monday morning 7 o'clock. I just finished my breakfast. Presume you would like to know what I had. In the first place I had one pint of coffee and sugar enough to sweeten it, a piece of boiled pork, two middling sized potatoes boiled, one loaf of light bread, salt and pepper.

I suppose you had a good deal better breakfast. I hope you had. I also hope you have plenty to eat and drink and wear. If you have not, you cannot blame, for I left you money enough to work on and I am perfectly willing for you to use all you want. First in order I shall write you on the happenings and welfare of you and children. In your last letter dated October 26 and 27 I received last Saturday, you stated for me to say whether I was willing that you should give Mr. Manning one dollar for Steepins [?]. Yes, I say and one more dollar with it if you like. Give all your conscience will allow you to give, for I sincerely think there are but very few that give freely enough for that good and Holy cause—to have the Gospel preached. I feel just as I have above stated.

You also requested me to say or give my consent whether you should buy that stove from Manning. I am very willing that you should get it. I think it very cheap at 4 dollars. I am perfectly willing for you [to] use all the money you want to make you and the children comfortable. I am not afraid of you going beyond anything, only what you necessary wants. Use judgment and economy, that is all I want, and I know you have never done anything else since we were married. Therefore, you see, the money I left you lays at your command. As regards myself, I aim to expend whatever for clothing or victuals, only paper, ink and stamps, envelopes, etc. (Tobacco, of course).

We will probably not get any more pay for 4 months yet, then we expect six months wages and one third more bounty, which in all will amount to $129. I intend to send home one hundred dollars, the balance I intend to keep for spending money. I am running pretty short of money now, but will have what will last me some weeks. I have 4 dollars left. I do not buy much but what I am obliged to, etc. Everything is three times as high here as in the North or where you live. Writing paper is 25 cents a quire [24 or 25 sheets of paper], envelopes two cents a piece. At them rates it wears away a few dollars of money. What used up my money so fast, I had to buy me a pair of boots, a gum blanket, suspenders, portfolio, ink stand, ink pens, etc. If you think of it when you write to me the next letter, put in a few dollars and I will pay you good interest for it when I get home.

Shafnocker, the man that married Robert's wife, is in our company. He is our cook. He requested me to state to you whether Bill Mier has got back from the West or not. I heard that Jasper Heagan has come back from Canada again.

Tomorrow is the day set for the great contest—who shall be the President. Old Abe or Little Mack. I hope and pray Mack may be defeated. Our regiment will pretty much all go for Lincoln. I am little afraid that Lincoln will be licked. By the time you receive this letter I presume we will know who is the man that has the finishing of this war. I hope to God it may come to a close in two months so we may all return to homes and families and live a Christian life the balance of our days on Earth.

Today it is raining but cold. Yesterday and Saturday night I stood picket on my post. We agreed amongst ourselves to stand 2 hours on and four off, so when I was off trick, I read my Testament. I opened my book in St. Matthew, the 27th Chapter and read.

You need not bother about them gloves. I can buy them here so that will save you the trouble, also save running the risk of them getting here. The letter I received from you on Saturday makes 6 I received from you. So there, you see, I have got all you wrote to me. I think I have written ten or eleven to you with one cent in each letter for Myron. In this letter I am going to send you a present which I made myself when I had not much to do. I made a finger ring out of a bone—a Virginia beef bone. I think it will just fit your third finger. It just fits my little finger.

The prospects at present are pretty good now for winter quarters here. If so, John Henry and myself want a box filled with nicknacks for winter, such as apple butter, baked or fryed apples, canned tomatoes, etc. We will write what we want. I must close for my sheet is filled. That paper you [sent] me never came. Send me a Star occasionally. Good day. Write soon. Be good girls and children. From your most affectionate husband,

Samuel Miller

November 14, 1864   Bermuda Hundred [Virginia]   #13

Don't show this. Write soon and often.

Dear and beloved wife,

I again take the opportunity of writing a few lines to inform you that I received your most kind and welcome letter dated November 5th. You also may be assured that I was very glad to hear you say you were well and had plenty to eat, drink and wear. If you have not, I certainly think it is your own fault for you live in the midst of a plentiful country.

The poor Reb soldiers in our front, that we can see every day, say that they only get one pint of flour or meal a day for their rations, and a piece of fresh beef one and half inches square, that is, they say so, them that come into our lines.

This is Monday. Saturday night and yesterday all day I was on picket. Last week there were 24 come to our lines Saturday night. One came across yesterday in broad daylight. One came over to us. He said that most all that was in the fortifications would come over but they dare not only as they can watch their opportunity and then they have to watch until them that [are] opposed to deserting get asleep and then they are off for our lines in a hurry.

I will give you an idea of our picket line on a piece of paper so you can see the position we are placed in, etc. I suppose you heard that General Sherman has burnt Atlanta. He is moving his army, that 70,000 men, upon Richmond. He has destroyed 30 miles of railroad and burns everything in his way, and if our Great Commanders are not fooled, Richmond and Petersburgh must fall before many days. Praise to God for it. Lincoln is elected again without any doubt. Thank God he is—for this cruel war will soon be over.

I am very hearty and am in good spirits and sincerely hope that we may soon return to our quiet home, where you cannot hear a constant firing of cannons. I have got so used to it that I do not mind it scarcely anymore.

Silence, send me the Tribune or Star occasionally. That one you sent me never came. You must be careful how you direct [them]—the same way that you do letters. You can also send small notions in those newspapers, that is, if you have anything of the kind to send. It will also save you little postage, etc. I received that Gum which was very good. I sent Myron two coppers. I sent in two letters. I also made a ring out of a bone and sent to you in a letter. The first opportunity I have I will have my likeness [portrait] taken and send home.

November 17th [continuation of the November 14 letter]

Since the above was written, I received another letter from you dated November 8 and mailed the 11th, which lay at your office three days before mailing. I also received the Star—its date November 3rd. I was very glad to get it.

I would have written when I commenced this, but there is so much duty and fixing for winter quarters that a man has scarcely time to eat, but will have it easier in a week or ten days. Tell Mrs. Hutchins that Frank has gone to Fortress Monroe to the hospital. He is getting better. Charles Swift is very low, is not expected to live just [much longer]. Tell Mrs. Jacob Brown of the fact. Also received them pills. You say you wish we could be sent back to Washington, but we will not get there this winter. One old colonel has come back from Washington. He says if we are good boys, perhaps by spring we may get there. I hope and pray by that time this terrible war will be over.

I received a letter from Ben the same evening I received yours. He is well and hearty. I wrote to you some weeks ago that Abner wanted fifty dollars. Let [him] have it until spring at interest as much as you can get—he only wanted it until spring. What has become of Hiram? I wrote to him a long time ago. Tell him for me, Silence, the first time you see him what he thinks of little Mack now?

You do not say anything how the weather is, etc. How does provisions rate in your country, how it sells, etc. Write all you can think of and a good deal more, that is, if you can think of them. John B. Henry is going to write home today also, and him myself are going to have you and Mr. Koury's folks send us a lot of things in a box together. I want one quart of apple butter; two or three pounds of butter; two pounds of cheese; some apples if you choose; some honey if you please; one pound of fine cut tobacco. Tell Mr. Ewing I want his best. Mark my things that you send me so we can tell them apart. Send just what you have a mind to and have Mr. Hervey send them to the Christian Commission.

I will here answer your questions that you ask me in your last letter—whether I liked you. Yes, I can say with all my heart. Think no other way—as long as you live. Did you wean Milo? I am well and hope you are and the children also are well. I pray for your welfare every day, etc. You need [not?] show this letter.

Samuel K. Miller

November 23, 1864   Camp Bermuda Hundred [Virginia]   #14

I received your letter dated November 14th. I was very glad to hear from you and children again. You said that you were getting along very well. I am pleased to hear you say so. I am also very well today. I took a bad cold laying on the ground at nights on picket. It settled in my back and has given me a diarrhea, but the doctor has given me some powder to take. He also excused me from duty. Otherwise feel very well.

We have had very wet weather for four days but think the rain is over for this time. I hope you and the children are enjoying good health. You wanted to know of me if I was willing that you should keep Mary Davis for company this winter. Yes, if she will stay, keep her, for she is company for you and is there all time. I don't think you can get any one that will suit you any better in the country. I am perfectly willing to have you keep her.

You said that you had got that stove. Now you want new pipe. Go to Masons and get all you want and be very careful that you make it very safe upstairs in the chimney that there will be no danger of fire. I have never thought at any time to write to you about my shop whether the neighbors bother you about the tools, etc. Don't let them carry them off. I am very glad that you can get your relief money.

I had a letter from Ben Ellis [Benjamin F. Ellis, Company K, 150th Pennsylvania, stationed in Washington, unit that guarded President Lincoln]. He is well. Also one from Enoch [Enoch Ellis, same location as Ben Ellis]. I wrote a letter to Hiram but he has not answered it yet. I received the Star. I also received one paper from David Russell. I have got all the letters you sent me.

I think the boys down at Petersburgh are going into it on the baby line. Let them go it while they are young. Well, in regards to myself, I think we have all the boys that we want. I shall send my likeness just as soon as I can get an opportunity. There is now one [photographer] here at present that takes them.

I have not much news to write, only there is prospects for a big battle before winter but [I] do not expect any fighting just along here. I wish the war was over for I long to get home to my family—if I am spared to go home I shall live a different life or a Christian life. I pray to my God every day that I might become a good Christian. I hope He may convert my soul to God. I am determined to serve my God. I feel better than I did when I left. I cannot read your letters without shedding tears. I hope I may return home again so you and myself can go to church together. I mean to buy a horse and buggy if possible. Remember me in your prayers and I will do the same with you. I suppose you have no bother getting bread stuffed. I think you will get along very well. Give my love to the others and a good share for yourself. I have a little book that I got from Christian Commission. It is a very good little book.

I think I must close for the present, hoping this may reach you in safety also find you in good health and spirits. I understand by a man that was home on furlough that there was good sleighing in Crawford County.

I must close expecting to hear from you soon again. Give my love to all that may inquire about me. From your most affectionate husband,

Silence, there is one thing I most forgot—is this. Selkirk Wade had a pair of boots made and sent to him and they were too small for him. I bought them of him. I am to pay him ten dollars. I gave him my note and the note he sent home to his wife. I want you to get the money and send it to her immediately. She lives at Linesville and [tell her] to send the note.

Samuel K. Miller

November 26, 1864   Bermuda Hundred [Virginia]   #15

I received your letter yesterday morning dated 20th of this month. I was glad to hear from you but was sorry to hear that Myron was not well. I hope he is not dangerous. I wrote a few days ago that I was not very well, but I have gotten well again. I only had a cold.

I will tell you how I took it and all about, for you will hear it at any rate, or see it in the newspapers. On last night a week ago the Jonnies made a break upon our picket line about half past 8 o'clock in the evening, with a strong force of two brigades which was about five or six thousand, so says their own newspapers. They come slipping upon us, the night being very dark and our line of works or picket line running the whole length through the timber, or woods, made it rather dark, or just before the moon rose. Well, they came within ten rods of us before they opened fire, which they done rather briskly. Nearly half of our boys had laid down to sleep and some had gone to sleep. I had set down by a little fire we had—off it went, bang-bang-bang it went all along the line. We all was ready in an instant, for we was expecting some move for several days that they had made their brags they were going to gobble our picket line. We, of course, thought they would give us some signs of it, but at all events, the thing is over and God spared my life. I thank Him for it.

The Rebs took our line with fifty-three prisoners from us, that is out of our regiment. They took our lines for eight miles. They took, in all, about 600 prisoners. There was one killed in our regiment, 3 wounded etc. There was 5 men in our post, there are 5 men in every post, and the posts are about as far apart as from the front of our house to the upper end of our garden. We all sprang to our rifle pits and commenced the combat, but their number being so much greater that ours, we were obliged to retreat but not until we gave them six or seven rounds. A great many of our boys left their rifle pits altogether. I tell you the Balls [minie balls] flew thick for about two hours. We stood to our post until the Rebs made a charge. I saw them first—then they was within 1 1/2 rods of us. The word was fire—so we did. We gave them five well aimed shots, then ran for the woods. The balls came whistling some then, but we all escaped unhurt. So it went. I will tell you all about it when I come home, Dear Wife.

Since the above has been written our regiment has been ordered to march to where I cannot tell, but will let you [know] in a few days where we will be. Silence, you may buy a new stove if you think the old one will not stand, but if I were in your place, I should buy one a size smaller. Do just as you please, Silence. Be contented with these few lines. I will write again in a few days. God bless you and children. Your husband,

Samuel K. Miller

December 1, 1864   **Army of the Potomac**
                             Front of Petersburgh [Virginia]   #16

Silence my dear wife,

Since I wrote you last we have done some marching. We got marching orders on last Saturday evening with 4 days rations. On Sunday about 10 o'clock we packed up our things and started but not knowing where we was or what place was destined for us—but at alevance [?] we marched 7 miles then encamped for the night. Next morning we started at daylight and marched all day reaching place of destination which being in all the distance of 21 miles. We only stayed for two nights then we got orders again to march with four days rations, taking back tracks for some point, but did not know where until we reached this place. We can see Petersburgh very easily from where we are encamped. I don't think we will stay here long, for General Meade does not want raw troops here. Therefore, I think we shant be here a great while. I hope to goodness they will take us from here, for there is not a more dangerous place on the whole front.

We had a hard march with our loads, the weather being very warm. The roads are dry and dusty. Oh, such weather I never saw in my life. The trees are green yet, but the country I do not like at all. You cannot see any person but soldiers now and then. You can see an old house with a family in it. Oh, it looks desolate and forsaken. I hope this war will soon come to a close. Sometimes I feel sad to see men standing and watching their fellow men with the weapons of war, and when the first opportunity affords itself, send them to Eternity with the content of your weapons. Oh, what a solemn thought if that should be my fate. I sincerely want to be ready to meet my maker.

You have asked me a serious question, in regards to my being converted or a child of God. I do not feel as though I have experienced religion, but I do feel as though I had an interest. I can say that I feel happy in my secret prayers to my God. I am determined to be a Christian. I hope you still pray for me a sinner. May God protect you and the children in your sleeping hours, etc. I wrote to you last Sabbath, that is, a part of it. I received that money. You need not send any more, I think. We will get some pay by the first of January. I will have four months pay due me then. If we leave here, I shall write to you.

There is some talk of getting a furlough to go home this winter. What shall I do, come home or not? I will only have to pay fare one way. If you see Hiram, tell him to write to me. Also, if Eliza [Samuel's sister Elizabeth (Miller) Mayo, usually called Eliza] says anything to you about that paper that I sent, it had a purpose to make her think of times that are past and gone. I think there will be a chance now to have my photograph. I expect you live fine on sausage now a days. Eat about one yard for me. I hope you will have no trouble in getting enough to eat.

You asked me whether I did not think you were improving to write. I think you have, very much. I can read your letters very well. I never received Doctor White's letter. Pay Jackson for them logs when he calls for it. Was Hiram satisfied with what money you gave him? I heard from you today by way of J. Henry. He got a letter from Nancy McQuiston stating Mr. Miller's family was well. I saw Billy Trimble yesterday. He is well and hearty. I also saw Jim Davidson and he is well, and Bob McMaster, they are fat.

Silence, I must close for it will soon be supper time. I hope you are all well and hearty. I am well and fat and hearty. Give my love to Mother and a great deal for yourself.

Good night, my Companion. Write when you can. Direct as you did before.

Samuel K. Miller

December 5, 1864   **Headquarters Army**
                              of the Potomac [Virginia]   **#17**

Affectionate companion,

I received your most welcome letter this morning, which found me in good health. I also was very glad to know that you and family were enjoying the weather. I am very glad that Myron has gotten better. I was afraid that he might be sick so long that he would be a great charge upon your hands, for I know that you would have enough to attend to, without any sickness, but we must take things as the Lord orders them.

Now you have asked me a few questions in regards to how we tent and wash, etc. Where we lay at present the shanties were built 7 by 10 feet, about 18 inches of ground dug out. First, the timber built up the same as a log house and the cracks dabbed up. We use the ground for floor and generally 4 to 5 in a tent. They are very damp and dirty. We are also damp and dirty. A very bad place for a man to be sick. There are a great many in our company that have the ague. John Henry chills every other day, but does not want his folks to know it, etc.

You wanted to know how much I owed John Rodgers—35 cents. I also owe McKee School Tax $2.95. I think that is what you wrote.

I received a letter from Hiram this morning. He writes that they are all well. He thinks this war will soon end because Abraham [Lincoln] was reelected. I think so myself, providing the Rebs accept old Abe's proposition. He gives them to the 8th of January next to do it in. If not, he intends to make another draft of one million more soldiers. I think that the way things are working at present it will come to a close soon. I think more than likely we will go to North Carolina if we move again.

I do my own washing. We made wash boards. There are plenty [of] camp kettles in our company, that we can have at any time to heat our water, then we take a pork barrel and cut or saw it in two pieces, which makes very good tubs. Then we go into it up to our elbows. Our shirts are easily washed but our drawers are cotton flannel, which get very dirty.

I am glad you have sent me a pair of socks. My socks that I brought from home are good yet, but those I got from the government are about worn out. I don't need any undershirts, the weather is so warm . . . . Oh, such lovely weather I never saw in my life! The roads are dusty.

Silence, how is Hiram's wife? Is she on the road for Boston again? How is it with you? All right, don't take no offense I must have a little sport with you! Myron, I will bring you a nice present when I come home for sending me those chestnuts. We will probably get the box next week if it does not go astray. There has been some 10 or 12 of our Company got boxes from home. Preacher Rodgers received one last evening Sabbath day.

I received a letter from Enoch yesterday morning, making inquiry whether I was taken prisoner. He had heard so. I did come very near being taken. The Rebs came so close to me that they halted me and four others, that we had to give leg bail [run] for our safety. The Rebs threw some 10 or 15 balls after us but fortunately did not take effect, but they came very close to our heads.

I was up to the sutlers [men contracted by the Army to sell merchandise to the soldiers] to buy some potatoes. I got two pounds, which cost me 20 cents. You wanted to know how we slept. When our two hours were off picket, we take our rubber blankets and spread them on the ground. We generally wear our overcoats then we lay down and snooze by the fire. Down where we came from we had to go on picket every other night, but where we are now we do not have anything of that kind to do.

The pickets where we are now fire at each other day and night. Their rifles are telescope seven shooters [rifles capable of shooting seven bullets without reloading], and all the way [the only way] they can get to their posts is through ditches dug in the ground 6 feet deep so the Rebs cannot see them going to and coming. We are drilled 3 hours every day. That is all the work we have to do until further ordered.

I lay around the shanty, read my Book, and write. The brass band is just playing a mournful piece—how solemn it sounds. May God bring this rebellion to a close and convert every soldier now in the field, for there are some awful wicked souls. I believe I have written all the news that would be of interest to you. I hope you and babies are well. I am well, also. If I have time I must answer Hiram's letter. Myron, get that ague shaken off you as soon as you can and be a good boy. To Milo and Mother and then I will bring you all something nice. Write as soon as you [can]. From your very affectionate friend,

Samuel K. Miller

**December 14, 1864   Army of the Potomac,
                          Petersburgh, Virginia   #18**

Dear Silence,

I received your letter of the 4th yesterday, which was the 13th also finding me in good health. The last time I wrote you we had marching orders. On Friday evening about dark we all pulled up stakes, as we called it, and started, but not knowing where, but at ever [any] rate, we marched about 2 miles and encamped for the night. And just about the time we barely got at pitching our tents for the night, it began to rain and snow and kept it up until morning daylight, when it ceased. We lay there all day.

In the meantime there were two men executed for desertion from our army to the Rebs. They were out of the 137th New York Volunteers. They deserted last July and [were] captured a short time ago. It was the hardest scene I ever beheld in all my travels. They were the boldest fellows I ever saw. One of them smoked a cigar upon the scaffold. The death warrant was read and then a prayer, then their faces were covered with white cloths, their hands and feet tied together and marched a couple paces to the front, and then the ropes adjusted about their necks, then the spring of the trap door was touched, which dropped quicker than flash. There they hung between Heaven and Earth. What a sight to see souls sent to Eternity! They never made any confession nor did they care where their souls went, for they were very wicked men. So that finishes that subject, with adding that there were about 13,000 present to witness the scene.

Now I will give you a full detail of our road we made, or were to have made. On Saturday evening about dark we pulled up and started for

the children, also Mother. Take care of yourself and babies. Write when you can. Sometimes I think I write twice a week but I write when I can. May this find you well. From your best friend. May God guard you in your sleeping hours.

Samuel K. Miller

December 18, 1864   Army of the Potomac [Virginia]   #19

Dear Wife,

I wrote you a letter a few days ago. Since then on the very next day we received our box. It was just nine days coming through. It also came in first class condition. John B. Henry is not with his company, therefore, he will not enjoy his nicknacks very much. He is sick at the hospital. The roast turkey was spoiled so much that it was not fit to eat. Everything else was very nice indeed. I am so well pleased with mine. You cannot imagine how I feel. Myron, I thank you a thousand times for them chestnuts you sent. Be a good little boy and be kind to Mother and I will bring you something very nice in return.

I have not opened anything, only one can of apple butter and can of tomatoes. The butter is nice but a little strong, but not any to hurt. I loaned half of it to those that are [not?] getting boxes from home.

We are now building our winter quarters. After we move I intend to open the honey and molasses. You spoke in your last letter that you did not think of sending cakes and bread. I am very glad you did not. Perhaps I will get you to send me some after while, but I will let you know when I want them. We generally get all the hardtack and soft bread that we want. Today we are boiling beans and fresh beef for dinner. This morning we had boiled potatoes and codfish, coffee and crackers, butter and sugar. So you see, we do not starve.

A week from today is Christmas. I wish I could be home on that day to help you eat a turkey. All I can do is to wish you a Happy Christmas. Remember that Santa Claus will be around—that Myron has his stockings hung up behind the stove. I presume you have cold weather there now. Last Sunday and Monday and Tuesday was very cold but since then the weather has been warm and pleasant. The roads are dry and nice. You would think it was fall weather.

The war is still going on. The Rebs are deserting daily by hundreds. General Butler has taken the railroad from the Rebs where we first lay at Dutch Canal, which is the last road they had between Richmond and Petersburgh. I do not see how they can stand it much longer. The impression of all [is] that the Rebs cannot contend longer than spring. I hope it may be so, for we are all tired of soldiers life, although I am not discouraged nor homesick or nothing of that kind. But it just seems to me as though we all should be home by summer, but I shall be contented with my lot—let it be what it may.

Silence, send me a late Tribune also do up handkerchief in it. Let me know how you get along in regard to wood, whether you made a wood hauling or not. There were 4 more deserters hung a few days ago at City Point. The health of our company is good at present. My health is very good. I am getting fat as a pig. I also hope you are well. Also, do your write to me every Sunday? Write to me often and give me all the news you can think of, and I will do the same. This is Sunday. We had regimental inspection this forenoon. This afternoon I am writing to an absent friend. We had no preaching to for what [reason] I am not able to tell. Last Sabbath we marched all day. You cannot hardly tell when Sunday comes.

Mr. Rodgers thinks there are some hard boys in our regiment. I think so myself. Rodgers knows you very well. I presume you know him, don't you? I believe he is a good man, or a Christian. May God convert my soul. I am resolved to try and try until I experience religion and be on the right side of my Maker. I feel earnest in what I say. I pray the Lord may spare my life to get home to enjoy the happiness with my wife and children the balance of my days. May God be with you and family always. Pray for me. Write soon and give all particulars. From your affectionate husband and well wisher. My love to you my friend. Tell Mother I send my best respects to her. Does Mary Davis still live with you? Let me know whether you have any cold weather or not. No more from your friend forever,

Samuel K. Miller

December 28, 1864   Army of the Potomac [Virginia]   #20

I received your letter mailed 10th last Sunday. Also received one from Brother Jesse. They were all well. I was very sorry to hear that Myron was sick again. You did not state in your letter what was the matter with him. I hope he may get along without giving you much trouble. I am very anxious to hear how he is getting along. I hope you and all are well, enjoying the hollowdays with abundance of good things. As my part I done very well considering where we are. We do not expect such things as folks do to home, but for all of that, I am content for the present. I hope in the future to enjoy myself better than ever heretofore if the Lord spares my life, which I feel within myself that he will.

Silence, I am not with my regiment any more. A week ago this morning, which is Wednesday, I was detailed by General Parks of the Ninth Army Corps of the Potomac to the Mounted Pioneer Corps. I will explain to you as well as I can what we have to do. In the first place we have horses to ride wherever we go if not more than one mile. There are 25 men in the company. Whenever there is a bridge to build or repair, we have to do it, also go with the provision train, help them through, fix bridges, etc. We carry no guns or arms of any kind for we will not be placed in any danger of the enemy.

The work is middling hard, but what signifies work if a man is in safety. This is a permanent detail for one year or more. I am well pleased with my position. The reason they detailed me was they wanted men that were steady and did not get drunk, etc. We just finished our cabin—are into it. This evening is the first night.

I would have answered your letter before but had no chance for the other tents were so crowded that I could not write. I wrote two to you not more than ten days ago. I shall write to you often now, for when our days' work is done we have no more to do until the next day. We never get up until 7 o'clock. We also have a man to do our cooking. All we do is to go to the cook shanty and get our plates and tin cups, get our grub and then go to our tents, eat and carry our dishes back and they are all washed and kept there until the next meal. We get soft bread every day, roast beef, sometimes fried pork, also baked beans. I have eaten my molasses and one can of apple butter. My butter, what I kept, is done, but I have four pounds loaned that I shall get back again in a few days.

The beauty of belonging to this Pioneer Corps is you have no luggage to carry. It is all hauled by our wagons that are in the corps. I was chosen as an axman. Some carry picks, some spades, etc.

Jesse writes that he has bought another farm on the road between Mercer and Georgetown. He also gets the Post Office. I have not heard from any of the rest of the friends. I cannot get my likeness here. We will go to City Point perhaps in a few days. If there is a possible chance to have it taken I will do so. I have not very much money at present but have some coming to me for the boots I sold. We also get pay 8th of next month, which will be $97 dollars. I shall send home $90 of it by Express. We all think of coming home by the first of May. The war is playing out. You would think so if you were here and see the Jonnies coming in every morning. Sherman has whipped them all out in Georgia. They all say there is no use to fight any more with the North. They also have sent peace men to Washington for peace. I hope and pray it may close tomorrow.

Silence, I will not write much this time, but will write in a few days. Try and do the best you can with the children, but I am really sorry to hear that Myron has had such a sick time this winter. Does the doctor think he is dangerous? Try and be content in your lonesome hours and trials. May God protect you and babies is my constant prayer for you—may we be unspeakably happy to be permitted to be together to enjoy ourselves again in each other society. May God guard you tonight from all harm. I hope you are well. I am well. Does Mother come to see you much? I want her to visit you every day. I shall write home more in the morning. Direct in plain writing.

S. K. Miller
Mounted Pioneer
Headquarters 9th Army Corps
Washington, D.C.

January 1, 1865   Headquarters 9ᵗʰ Army Corps [Virginia]   #21

My dear wife,

A happy new year. May God protect you in my absence during this year. This is New Year morning, one o'clock I presume. You may wonder what has me up at this time of the night. I am not speaking like I used to do in Old Pennsylvania. I will tell you I am on guard watching our horses, they do not kick each other or get untied and run about and tear up Ned. There are 41 head in all, in and about the stable. It requires two of us every night to stand guard or rather watch them. My turn comes every 11 or 12 nights. The balance of that time at nights I get my sleep. I think I have such a good place. I have no marching and nap sack to pack upon my back or a gun to carry. Our luggage is all handled for us and we are on our horses' backs. I have a good horse, saddle and bridle and when we go and come from our work, we make the horses git. They are all fat and feel nice, etc. So be content. I think I was very lucky to get here. I presume it is all for the best, or at least I hope so.

Tonight it is very cold, freezing, the ground is white with snow but I am comfortable. I have a first rate warm shanty with a good fire place and a roaring big fire. My mess mates are fine men. Both from Pennsylvania. One is a young man. The other is married. Both [were] detailed the same time I was—one from my regiment, the other from the 208ᵗʰ regiment. All came out when we did. The single man's name is Huston and the other Bookhamer.

I got a letter [from] John Miller Petersburgh [Ohio] the same time I got yours. He writes they are all well. Also states Isaac Miller sold out where he lives and has bought a house and a lot at Sharon [Pennsylvania]—paid two thousand dollars for it but would not tell me what business he intends going into. He said he would let me know the next letter he wrote.

How I would like to see Milo walk, the lazy little scamp, and see them teeth and fat face of his. I expect that he is a captain. Myron, if I had been to home I should have been into them stockings of yours. Just wait until next Christmas. I will get some candy, too, in my socks! Do you think old Santy Claus will give me some or will you save me some of yours? I am sorry that you did not get your flannel woven for you a dress this winter, but I guess you will stand it, for you are pretty fat and warm. You will have to wear the more calico. I don't want you to freeze yourself when you have plenty to get with. I will tell you, sleep close to Mead [Milo], he will keep you warm at nights and my old woman will through the day.

You stated that there was such good sleighing. I think if I was there that you and I should have a ride if I had to buy a horse to go with it. I suppose Dow and wife are improving the snow. How does Mag seem to flourish this winter buying remnants and making flying squirrel's aprons? Is she the good natured or not? Does your mother go there any? When you answer this inquisitive letter, lay it before you or you cannot answer all my questions that I demand of you. Don't think hard what I say. You better be careful about using so much paper writing to me or I shan't buy you another dress. Ain't you afraid that old Benona Ewing can't supply you in paper?

If old Ben ever asks you anything about me, tell him I said that we are going to put an end to this Rebellion by spring. All we ask is for Sherman to clean them out of Georgia and old U.S. Grant and his army hold the Rebs here at Richmond. By next spring they will all desert. They only come at the rate of 20 and 25 of a night to our headquarters, besides what comes in at other places all across the lines, a distance of about 40 miles.

Give Mr. Ewing my best respects if you please. Has John Hay been around assessing yet? Did you have our valuation cut down any? I think old Loring [Mayo] and family have jumped out of the frying pan into the fire in regards buying farms, but anything in the shape of dirt will do them for they love dirt. The reason I sent her that paper, I expected she would write to me and acknowledge some things to me. I rather think she feels guilty. I shall send her another religious paper, the first I get. I sent you a letter day before yesterday in answer to the one I received Christmas Day and this one in answer to the one yesterday. Write as often as you can, give me all the news for I like to hear from home. I believe I have written all the news that will be interesting to you. I am well and hearty. I hope this may find you and the family all well and enjoying the best of health. My best wishes for your welfare. May God be with you and guard you in your sleeping hours. Let me know what Joseph McQuiston is doing this winter. Also whether Frank Hutching is or was home. I must close. Expecting to hear from you soon. My love to you and children. Also another—do you ever hear from Alfreda? I must write to them.

I love you, too.

Goodbye, my Dear,

S. K. Miller

Direct to Samuel K. Miller
Mounted Pioneer
Headquarters Ninth Army Corps
Washington, D.C.
Samuel K. Miller (in plain writing)

Silence, I almost forgot. I was just eating a piece of bread and apple butter and some cod fish. I am finishing the second can. I tell you it is good in old Virginia. It is now between 4 and 5 o'clock. The Bugle horn started blowing, the drums are a beating. The pickets are firing to keep the Jonnies from charging upon our lines. Now and then you can hear a cannon go chabung. The world here is all in commotion. Every man knows his duty. It seems hard that men have go stand for years in the cold and wet to watch the treacherous Rebels. I hope God will stop this terrible war, let men return to their respective firesides with wife and dear children. I cannot help feel affected when I write, nor can I hear a man talk of such things but the tears come to my eyes. I do not know what is the reason, but that is the way I feel.

Good morning, Silence. How do you do? My New Year's gift. Also a Happy New Year and a pleasant one. I thought I should write more today but nothing has happened worth mentioning. We were out to the railroad station to repair a platform, but no timber to do it with, so we rode back to camp. The weather is nice today, a little cold, but not as cold as it is probably in Penna. I am well and hope you enjoy good health. From your affectionate and well wisher. Take care of yourself. Give me all particulars, the weather and prices of muslins, etc.

Goodbye, my Dear,

S. F. Miller

January 8, 1895   **Headquarters Army**
                             of the Potomac [Virginia]   **#22**

Dear Wife,

I was just down to my regiment, a distance of one mile. Expecting a letter from you. I am very happy today. I was not disappointed as you said you were. Oh, how I was pleased to hear that you were all well again, for I was very uneasy about Myron not getting along. I am also happy to say the Lord is blessing me with good health. I thank Him for it daily. I pray that He may watch and protect me all my lifetime.

Well, I just finished my dinner and watered my horse, so I will endeavor to scribble a few more lines to you. I have not much news to write today. I wrote you a letter last Sabbath and one a few days previous to that. I am sorry that you did not get more wood cut the day of your frolic after going to so much bother in preparing for it. The next one you make, don't calculate it so far ahead. Make it when the snow is good or the weather is nice. But however, I suppose you did the best you could under the circumstances. I find no fault whatever, for I calculate you to wear the britches while I am gone. I know you will manage things well enough.

Yesterday and last night and today is cold and chilly but the sun shines bright and pleasant. The roads are pretty good yet, owing to the weather. Thomas Gitchel and Lyman Kilgore were over to our regiment yesterday to see the boys, but I did not see them. Tom was up on a furlough to see Lyman. His regiment lays upon our left, probably four miles. I think more than likely that he will come to see me before he goes back.

Silence, what does the people think about the coming draft. Are they making any preparation to meet it, or do they intend all to skiddadle for Canada, or hire Rebel substitutes as they did before. I think I done or took a wise plan in coming when I did, for it certainly would have caught me this time if I had not been drafted before. On the other hand, if I had not come I should have been kept poor by paying out money all the time trying to raise volunteers. So I think I am making money by coming and, if the Lord spares my life, I can enjoy it when I get home, and that in such a way that it will please God and man.

I wrote a letter to Hiram, one to Jesse and one to John at Petersburgh, and this one makes three to you in ten days or twelve at the farthest. If I had the time I should write to you every other day, but I will write to you as often as once a week at the extent. I would like to write to Abner but I do not know if it is of any use, for you can tell them all where I be and what I am doing.

I like my position first rate, only we have to work some days pretty hard, but otherwise we can rest at night and Sundays. I read a few chapters in the Testament today. We have a nice little log hut, warm and comfortable and a good bunk to sleep on. Everything nice as can be expected.

I received the Tribune and the handkerchief and am very much obliged to you until better payed. I will send you my likeness [portrait] just as soon as I get my pay. If that does not suit you I will bring you present when I come.

Direct Samuel K. Miller
Mounted Pioneer
Headquarters Company, 9th Army Corps, Washington, D.C.

The news came to headquarters that Sherman has taken Charleston, but I thought [it] doubtful. What does George McGranahan think about the war now—also about the draft? I can tell you the reason you did not get more wood cut—because you are an abolitionist wife. What do they think now about me going to the Army? I would like to talk to some of them Copperheads, as I think I could tell them some things that would not set very well on their stomachs. Silence, how do you get along sleeping alone? Don't you wish for me some nights, with my cold feet? (Nonsense!). I am well. I hope you are, too. Kiss the babies for me.

From your husband

Samuel K. Miller

January 15, 1865   **Headquarters Army**
                              of the Potomac [Virginia]   **#23**

Dear Affectionate Companion,

I received your letter last evening dated 8th. This is Saturday evening. I was very glad to hear from you. Much more so to hear you say that you were all well. As regards myself, my health is very good at present. In the first place I suppose I can prepare myself to answer some questions, which I will do willingly. The first question (in program you wanted to know) is whether there is any church here. I am sorry to say there is none nearer than our regiment. Secondly you wanted to know how far I was from the regiment. It is just about one mile. Thirdly and lastly I get no more wages than I did when in the regiment. I am satisfied with my position, better than if I was getting twenty dollars per month. The work is harder. My souls, what signifies work when a man has a good horse to ride to and from his work. We never go to work until nine o'clock or after and then come in for dinner and then quit before sundown. Then all you have to do—feed your horse, eat your supper, set around your shanty and go to bed when you please.

My things you sent me all came safe and in good order. I will tell you how John Henry's things came to be stolen or rather eaten up. A few days before our box came, John was taken to the hospital sick. He gave a mess mate of his by the name of Robert Swartout from Meadville orders that when the box came to take charge of it and eat what he wanted. And so he did, eat everything but three cans of fruit and some butter. The balance he either ate or gave away. So if the Henry's folks ever say anything to you about it to you, you can tell them that is the way his things were stolen.

Yes, when I send you my money you may have your photograph taken. I shall send to Meadville or Jamestown, but I will let you know where I will send it to. Tell Jason Bard if he wants a letter any plainer directed then I do yours, I will write it in capital letters. I don't like to lean so much to the right—I always like best to the left. Yes, the moon shines very nice and clear. I almost wish sometimes that I would like to be at home to see it shine against the front side of our house.

I think you need not send me any more things, only one thing—and that is a hat. I want you to go to Mr. Ewing. Tell him to send me one by mail. I don't want a black one or a red one. Something like my old one I had. I don't want it cost over a couple of dollars, if you can get one for that. I cannot get one here for less than 6 or 7 dollars. Tell him to do it up in paper, send by mail, and I will pay him when I come home. You can tell about the size by my old straw hat. Send it immediately, for I am as black as an Indian with my little blue cap on.

I wrote a letter to Charley this week. I wrote him an awful long letter—give him all the war news I knew, etc. Silence, if my old buckskin gloves are not lost and are whole, put them in my hat and send them, too.

I am sorry you got a calf for a man. I suppose she [this seems to refer to Mag, or Margaret Rudy Ellis, wife of Abner Ellis. Samuel seems to speak not very kindly of her in these letters!] thinks she got a bull for a man, or else she would have so many young ones. I think that is what is to matter with her now. She is mad she will have a calf. If I had not more sense than she has got, I would go and exhibit myself as one of the old John Rudy's [Margaret Rudy Ellis's father] griners [steers]. Let her talk. She can't hurt you or me, for I consider her beneath my notice. She will think I am a calf when I get home. She better not brag. Abner may have to come to war yet before it is finished. Oh, I shan't waste ink and paper talking about her. She is a poor, silly fool, but I like to have you write about what she says about me.

I was just over to the regiment. Expected to get a letter from David Russle, but did not get any. I saw all the boys but John Henry. He is at the hospital again. We have not been paid off yet but expect to every day. If we are not paid now, we shan't be until the first of March. Our _____ said that the 5th Corps will be paid tomorrow. If that should be the case, the whole army will be. When you direct the next letter to me don't put an "eye" into the word Mounted. It is [a] plain and easy word [to be] spelled. I have not been out much last week to work. I stayed at camp and shaved shingles for the Lieutenant's cabin. So you see I am somewhat favored by being a mechanic. I am very well and hearty but cannot sleep all night. I am generally up in the morning about 4 o'clock reading my Testament. I have commenced to read it through. I am about halfway through Mark. I hope you are well and the boys too. May God be merciful with you to guard and direct you—is my prayer. Write soon as you can. Give my love to all that inquire about me. No more from your husband. This I have finished today. Myron, be a nice boy and I will remember you when I come home.

Silence, I wish you would send me a few stamps for fear that we will not get our pay. I have money coming to me, but I may not get it soon.

Samuel K. Miller

| **January 24, 1865** | **Headquarters Army** | |
| | **of the Potomac [Virginia]** | **#24** |

Dear Wife,

I received your letter this morning, dated 15th. Our mail was detained on the River two days on account of a very heavy fog. I was very glad to hear that you were all well and trying to get along as well as you are, etc. As regards to my health it is very good at the present. I also received a letter from Almira and Mary Mayo [Samuel's nieces, daughters of his sister Elizabeth Miller Mayo. Almira was 17 years old and Mary 22 years old at that time] this morning. They let on in their letter to be wonderfully concerned about me, how I get along and how I spent the Hollowdays and how much George Donaghy [Elizabeth's son-in law, husband of another daughter Emaline] was offered for their property—five thousand dollars, and did also tell that they had bought a farm, etc.—and I was going to turn their whole attention to making cheese. That Mrs. Mayo was very sick or had been, and that she sent her love to me. I never, never was so surprised in my life when I got the letter! I knew they would come to milk after a while, but old Loring [Mayo] never said yes or nay.

I have some of a notion to answer the letter. They also wanted my likeness, but that they cannot have—to finger about. I intend to have about 4 photographs taken just as soon as we get our pay. That may be perhaps not until the first of March coming. I can have my face taken at our headquarters. I want you to write in your next letter how I should have it taken, whether with a musket or without. I am just out of money and I owe Enoch 50 cents for postage stamps. I have about seven or eight dollars but cannot get it until they get their pay also. I don't know but I must dun you for a couple dollars. That will be all that I want for the time. I do hate to send for money, but I must have paper and ink and stamps and tobacco or I must quit writing letters. You wanted to know whether I could have the privilege of going to Washington. I think hardly unless the war should come to a close between now and the 4th of March.

Silence, if you can get Mary Davis to stay with you next summer, keep her, for you cannot get a girl that will suit you any better. I think she can earn pretty near her board—and if she can't it is worth more than her board for company. Have her stay if she will. Tell her I said so. I hope you enjoyed yourself at the Oyster supper at Adamsville and I suppose you paid for it, too. Be careful that you do not eat too many for they have a bad effect.

Oh, how I would like to be home to take a sleigh ride! The day you wrote this letter you sent me, I was down to my regiment, and a prettier day I have never saw. Last Sunday was a beautiful day. The sun shown all day, warm and pleasant. You wanted to know how I spend my Sundays or at least the Sunday of the 15th. I spent it in reading my Book—that I keep for my Guide. I love to read it more and more every day. I would like to know what mouse that was that brought you that corn, but I will bet that you did not get it for nothing. I am getting a memorial of our company. It is a very nice picture with all the names of our company. It will cost $1.50. Myron, I will send it to you. I want you to take good care of it, and keep it clean and when I come home I will frame it. I will get it in a week or ten days, then I will send it by mail.

This Wednesday morning about 4 o'clock I got tired sleeping and laying so I thought that I would spend an hour or so in writing to one that I love dearly. While I am writing the gun boats are throwing their deadly shots at each other down on the James River. Night before last the Rebs made an attack upon us down on the James at the Dutch Canal where we lay last fall, but the Rebs were badly whipped. We sunk two rams [Confederate ships reinforced with iron bows in order to pierce the wooden hulls of Union ships, thereby rendering them inoperative] for them and blew up one and disabled two. The Rebs have made the second attack and what the result will be this time we know not.

Silence, the war is coming to a close fast, so writes Enoch. I had a letter from him a few days ago. Keep in good cheer. We shall soon see each other again, if not until the expiration of my year, that is fast wasting away. Fret not about me. I will take care of myself, also of my Soul. I pray that God will see me safe home again to my beloved little family. I hope you will enjoy yourself sleigh riding, for we have no sleigh riding here. But nicer weather you never saw. Tthis morning the ground is frozen hard but clear. May God be ever with you and family. I hope you are all well. I am well and I don't have to work very hard. Write often and I will the same. I expect to hear from you. Send my love to Mother, etc.

Let me know when you write again how many dishes of oysters you ate. Write all the particulars and about the draft and what our township is going to do for the call. Tell Meg that now is her chance to send her man to war, then perhaps she can get a remnant for a dress.

From your dearest, kind husband. Write soon. Good morning.

Samuel K. Miller

January 26, 1865   Headquarters 9th
                          Army Corps [Virginia]   #25

Dearest,

This is Thursday morning about 3 o'clock. The shanty got cold. I thought I would get up and put on a fire. I sat a while and warmed my shins and toasted two slices of bread and ate them with honey on them. My honey is about done, which is the last I have that you sent me. I have received two letters from you this week, one last evening and one Tuesday morning. Which I was very glad to hear from you. So you see, I was glad twice in one week.

I cannot sleep more than six or seven hours. I get so sore and tired that I must rise and put on a fire. The weather now is cold and clear, but no snow, but will only last a few days. Although the days are pleasant and warm, the nights are frosty, which is the reason our shanties get cold. The walls are tight and warm, but our roof is nothing but tent cloths or heavy drilling [heavy, thick mud often used for drilling holes into the earth]. They turn rain Bully but are cold. That is the way the soldiers' houses are all built throughout the army. The earth all along our lines are dotted with just such houses and inhabited with Uncle Sam's boys, also in places for two miles back in the rear of the lines.

We lay very near two miles in the rear of the front, but we can see the Reb shells explode and hear the pickets firing. I just wish you could be here and see the position the Army of the Potomac lays in. You would think the soldiers had hard times and would get sick and tired living 3 years in the army, but they all like it. For my part I like it middling well, if it was not for being deprived of society and comforts of life at home. But I pray the expiration of my year will find me sharing the comforts and society with my wife and children.

Myron, I want to say a word to you. Will you not send Pap your little likeness, that small one without the case, the next letter Mother writes to me? All the rest of the married men in the Pioneer Corps have their little boys and girls pictures to show. I want yours to show also. I know that you are as pretty as any I have seen, yet you must not forget to send it. I will bring it home again. I have a nice picture that I am going to send to you. I received the letter where you stated what ailed Myron, also about how [many] bushels of potatoes you had, etc.

Do you want to know how many Jonnies came to our lines since the first of this month? I will tell you, so you can tell the Copperheads. There were five hundred and seventy, amongst them were two women from the city of Petersburgh. One of them was dressed in black silk, the other black calico, so you see, she must be a rich man's wife. The Rebs are about starved out. They only get quarter rations, so they say, that deserts to our lines. I stated in my letter to you to keep Mary if she will stay. Make yourself and children comfortable.

I am not going to tell you as Ben told Mary to swing and cut a great splash. You know I want—cut according to your cloth, etc. I know too you will do it without my telling you. Them oysters you ate of mine, I tell you they were good. I would have been afraid to sleep with you that night for I know they had a bad affect on you. I am heartily glad you was down. I hope [you] enjoyed yourself, also. It was for a good cause.

How does Dow [Lorenzo Dow Ellis, Silence's brother] and his wife flourish these times, and Mag, and Mary, Ben's wife? Tell him to write to me, and I will write him the longest letter he ever read. Don't forget to tell him. I suppose you have sent me that hat I wrote for. I have not much more to write. I am very well and hope you and the family are also. Write when you can. I will do so also. I am still making shingles right by my shanty. I hardly ever go out with the boys to the woods or on the road to work. Our sergeant is going home this week on furlough. Then we will have good times. I have a fine spirited horse, and [he is] a nice rider. He can jump a ditch or log just like a rabbit. So I must close for this time. Silence, good morning. I think I shall lay down and snooze a while longer. The fire is good and warm. Now, from your husband.

Samuel K. Miller

February 1, 1865   **Headquarters 9th**
                          Army Corps [Virginia]   **#26**

Dearest companion, Don't show this. Keep to yourself.

I received your letter the 26th also the hat and gloves and stamps. I thank you to the bottom of my heart for your kindness and trouble which I am constantly putting you to. I do not know whether I can every repay you again. I hope in the end to spend my days with you, a true Christian and a loving husband and a Christian father. That is my full determination. I pray whenever I have an opportunity to my God to spare my life and spare me to return home again with my dearest.

I am very well at present and sincerely hope and pray that you all enjoy good health. There is a strong talk of a peace settlement. May God grant it may be so. Vice President Stephans Hunter and Campbell are at

Washington to see whether there is a hope for peace. They came across the picket line opposite Petersburgh and was escorted by General Parks in a four-horse carriage to Meade's station where they took the cars for City Point, thence by water to Washington. If they do come to any terms of peace, the war will end in a couple months. Then, in all probability, us new troops will be home by the first of May. You can tell the people if they doubt this news, tell them it is so, for there was one of our boys saw the man come to Meade's station. Troops are all anxious to hear of peace once more. (I say amen to it!)

Silence, I am making candles last night to bed time and today. I have made three dozen and have tallow enough left to make 6 or 8 more. We borrowed moles from a Reb family that lives within our lines, and the tallow we can get all we want by going for it where they kill beef cattle off—from the guts. The government never pretends to save the tallow. The guts are all buried. So I will have candles enough to read and write all I want. You said that you dare not write your feelings for fear of making me feel sad. I do love to have you write your feelings for I feel that the Lord is on my side. I know He is. I am not inclined to break his commandments. I do know that I love to read my Testament better than I ever did. Oh, how I wish this war might close and let me go home. I am not discontented or homesick, but I want some one to kneel down with me and pray for me, and ask for forgiveness.

Your letters I have burnt them all but for eight. If we stay in camp I shall save them until spring, then I will burn them. There is no one sees them for I keep them locked up in my portfolio but when I read them over two or three times I burn them. I had a letter from Hiram a few days ago. He did not write anything that was interesting to me—only said that you and your Mother was there on a visit. He talks of putting up his house next summer and getting it enclosed and then have me finish it for him. I have not answered his letter yet. I have answered Almira Mayo's letter. I gave them some sly rubs, too. I have just finished my dinner. We had fryed beef and pork and hard tack.

We have not had much to do now, only chop wood and burn it. Our sergeant has gone home on a furlough. So we have good times now, only lay around. I only hope we may remain our time out. Myron, I suppose you have fine times playing with your sled. I suppose you still have your cart not broken yet. Silence, have you your stove set up in the room yet? How much money is there in Ewing's stove? I want to have about five hundred dollars in money when I get home. I want to finish my house and dig a cellar, and buy some hardware at Pittsburgh when I come and some groceries, too. I [have] not much more to write. Only I hope we may both be good Christians in our old days. Pray for me. I expect to hear from you again soon. Give my love to all that inquire about me. Write soon as you can. Did old Ben like to trust me? Does he ever inquire about me? I still remain your best friend on Earth. Keep in good spirits for a few months more.

From yours very respectfully.

Samuel K. Miller

This Sunday 12 degrees and very windy and cold from the Northwest and we had to work all day making roads which went very much against my will, but what are we to do when we are ordered to work. I don't think we will have to answer for it in the day of Judgment. I hope you have spent the Sabbath Day differently. This letter starts for you in the morning.

You would think if you were here this evening it was snowing to see the white sand fly in the air. I never saw it blow much harder in my life. It makes our shanty flutter, but we can keep it warm. Write soon if you please. My love to all that may want to hear. I answered Mol Mayo's letter but I shan't write to them again.

February 9, 1865   Headquarters 9th Army Corps [Virginia]   #27

Dear wife and children,

This is Thursday morning about one o'clock. I am upon Guard the after part of the night and a beautiful morning it is too. The moon shines bright as day. I have not had a letter from you since the one written January 25th. I answered it immediately and would have wrote since then but expected one, but have been sadly disappointed every night's mail. So I could not stand it any longer. I presume tonight I will receive one, but if I do I shall answer it right off.

There has been a great battle in progress upon our left. The Rebs made a move in that direction with the intention of breaking our lines, but was severely whipped by the fifth Corps which took the South Side railroad, but were repulsed, but our boys rallying again and retook the Road and are holding and fortifying it. I have not heard our loss or the Rebs, but I will let you know in my next letter. My regiment is out, but was not engaged in the battle. There were 70,000 men there but only one corps engaged, which is about 30,000. The Rebs said to our boys when they got there—Yanks, you will get what you come for—but I think it was the reverse. They got what they didn't want, a good whipping. The intention of Grant is to take the Danville Road, then the Rebs will have to evacuate Petersburgh. Them were the only two roads they had to get their supplies on for their army. I think if they get several good thrashings they will come to terms of peace.

The weather here at present is cold and wet, or has been for several days past, but has cleared off. Pleasant again. We still remain where we was, but we did not know how soon we might get marching orders to fall back behind the breastworks of City Point. There is always the place our wagon trains and the Mounted Pioneer goes until after the battles. This fight about which I have spoken was about 12 miles to our left, or in other words, due South.

I still keep well and hearty. Not much to do. I hope you are all well. I almost fear that some of you are sick, the reason that I have not had a letter, but I trust and pray that you are all well.

I am very proud with my hat and gloves you sent me. The hat was a little larger, but I laid some paper under the lining, which makes it just right. I see old Ben had it marked 3.00 dollars. How do you get along about wood this cold weather? Have you plenty, and how does the old remnant get along and feel about the draft? By this time, she may stand a chance to get a new dress this spring. Let me know about whether Findley McQuiston was enrolled in the draft and what the Township intends doing in regards to filling their quota.

This is Thursday evening. I received the long looked for letter this evening, which has relieved my mind of anticipated trouble at home. I feared some of you were sick or something wrong, but as I said above, I am at rest again. I feel happy and more. I will also state that the five dollars was also in the letter. That must last me until we are payed off, which will be the 10th of March, without a doubt. I also hope that by that time the Rebs will come to the conclusion to come back into the Union. I have prophesied all winter this thing will be settled this spring. I feel it within me and I cannot give it up. I was just thinking this morning to myself when I was writing this letter how old remnant was getting along I think from a fool _____ [There are three lines which Samuel wrote are crossed out here] for luck and a poor man for children. It also seems to be Ab's luck at alavence (?).

You say you received five dollars more of relief money. You say it seems like a gain. I think so myself, and a considerable gain. If I do pay a certain portion by tax, I don't think I have to pay 50 cents a year toward it. Did not you not say that you lost two months pay in the start? You ought to of had pay for five months, which would make 25 dollars. It does not matter much either way. All I have to say—take all you can get. I think I am entitled to it.

I have not received any letter from Charley's folks yet. I do no know why they do not answer my letter. Perhaps they never got it. I also wrote Jesse about the same time and have not got an answer yet. Silence, when you are to town and think of it, ask David Russel whether he ever answered my letter. If not, tell him to direct to the Mounted Pioneer Corps. [The reason] I wanted to know was this—our company clerk has opened a great many letters for different ones that was directed to the company, expecting to contain money.

One thing I almost forgot—when you answer this letter tell me how you make codfish gravy. We frequently have them and the only way we can cook them is boil them. Don't forget to write how you do it. I do not think you want to see me any worse than I do you.

I would give 25 dollars to be home this spring. I dream of home of late but am always disappointed when I wake up. The time is advancing fast when I shall see you all again and enjoy your company and take the place of a Christian father and husband. This is my full determination if God preserves my life, which I hope He will. I am well and hearty and I pray for the preservation of you all. Answer this as soon as possible. I believe I have written all I can think of. Hoping to hear of your good health. My respects to you all.

Yours very truly forever,

Samuel K. Miller

February 11, 1865   **Headquarters 9th**
                             Army Corps [Virginia]   **#28**

Silence, my dear,

This evening I received your letters of the 3rd and 5th which found me in good health and was much pleased to hear that you were all well. I did intend not to answer this until tomorrow, but Colonel Pierce came home this, or rather back from home on furlough. Coming from the station he observed several bad bridges, which he ordered repaired tomorrow. Therefore we have got to work whenever the order is given, although he is not a man that wants his men to work on the Sabbath Day. But the road is almost impassible for teams where there are hundreds of them have to cross every day, etc.

I wrote to you day before yesterday. I also stated in my last letter that there was a great battle upon our left. Our regiment was called out but was not in the fight. The 5th and 6th Corps done all the fighting, and whipped the Jonnies very bad. We advanced our line two miles and lengthened it six miles and built breastworks sufficiently strong enough to hold them at bay. The Rebs charged the 5th and 6th three times but were repulsed each time with a heavy loss. Our loss in killed was about 200 and wounded was about double the number of killed. Lyman Kilgrove was in the battle, I think. He either belongs to 5th or the 6th Corps, I cannot say which. Also, Jim Davidson, William Trimble, William McMaster, William McQuiston, Robert Bowden, Wallace Brown, but I think they all escaped unhurt, or at least I did not see any of their names on the list of wounded. The Rebs seemed to be down on peace nowadays. They cry—fight it out—or independence to the last. I think Grant will give them all they want by the time the roads get settled in the spring, if not before.

Tell Aunt Carry I have [not] seen Jim since last fall. Therefore cannot tell her anything concerning him in regard to drinking or gambling, but I should say that he does not look like a man that made use of strong drink and gambling. I know nothing about it, but you can tell her the army has not been payed off since the first of September last, and if he does gamble and drink, he has not spent more than 3 months pay. I think I shan't ask you to [go to] the bother of sending me any more apple butter, etc. They cost not much, I know, but the trouble in getting them to railroad is more than I can ask of you to do. I think you have done more now in sending me one thing and another than I can ever pay you for. We cannot tell how long we may remain here. We are liable to move from here at any moment or any hour. I think I can live on Jack beans and pork a few months more very well. I thank you very much for what you have done.

I also think that you had not better take any boarders. I will give you my reasons for why. Not that I fear it would raise a talk, or anything of that kind, but I don't think it would pay, for everything is high, and too much trouble for a woman in seeing to get provisions and etc. Furthermore, we are not prepared with bedding, etc. Tell Abner for him to board them. He may need a little money to buy his wife a cloak. Silence, if you hear of a chance to bargain with some of the old women in the country for goose feathers, do it. Tell them to have them ready for you by fall coming. I think, then, feathers will [be] cheap.

If the boys will give you the wood for hauling, I think the best thing you can do is to hire someone. If you have, pay them the money. Get it done. I think Ralston would be a good hand if you can hire him. Then get someone a day or two to haul. I want you to work the machine yourself and make yourself comfortable as you can and I will not find any fault whatever. Do just as you think best and I will be satisfied—without asking me. I know you will do for the best all the time.

Good morning, Myron, how do you do? I hardly expected to see you in Dixie. How do you like Virginia among the Jonnies? Yes, I shall take good care of you. Your pretty picture has not come yet, but look for it every day and just as soon as it comes to me, I shall send it to you. I just gave you a sweet kiss. Be a nice boy and kind to Mother, and God will love you for he loves little children. He loves everybody, even to the black man.

Silence, it is getting late. I have written almost all that is of any importance and sincerely hoping you all well. God be within you and family. Silence I cannot help but saying something to you about the goodness of our Savior. I feel so. I cannot saying something about _____. You always have my best. Warmest wishes for your welfare in my absence. Peace be with you. May the guardian angels hover around your pillow in your sleeping hours. Good night, write often. My love forever,

Samuel K. Miller

February 19, 1865   Headquarters 9ᵗʰ
**   Army Corps [Virginia]   #29**

Dear Wife,

I received your letter this morning of the 9ᵗʰ, which met a kind receptance. I was also very glad to hear from you all, and more than pleased, yes, happy to hear of your good health which is a great blessing. How slightly we do appreciate it, nor do we scarcely thank our Heavenly Father for those blessings which is constantly given to us poor wicked sinners. Lord, convert my soul, is my daily prayer. I hope my prayers may be answered. I am not in the least discouraged. Yet. My health is good. Thank God for it.

My dear companion, pray fervently for me. I hope the time is not far hence when we shall enjoy the privilege of being together again, to spend our days in serving our Redeemer. May God grant it

I think from what we can learn in the newspapers peace is at no great distance off. South Carolina talks strong of coming back into the Union. Since the peace commissioners accomplished nothing in restoring peace to our land, desertions is more rapid than ever known before. Yesterday

20 Rebs came to our lines with there arms and equipments, perfectly resistless, and said they thought it useless to fight, for they were a whipped nation. I saw five pass when to work on a bridge. We asked them whether they had any late news from General Sherman. Yes, they said. They heard that he had captured Columbia and they got scared and thought it best to come to us.

Desertion is a common occurance nowadays. I still think by the first of May or probably in April will see peace. I say "amen" to it.

Silence, I want you to ask someone who knows as whether there is an Adams Express Office at Meadville. But I think that there is, but I am not sure, but you find out and let me know in your next letter. You wanted to know whether I wanted some more things sent in a box. I think it will hardly pay so late in the winter. There is no telling how long our corps may stay here, and all the boxes that are sent to soldiers are opened and a great many things in the boxes are eaten by the poor swell head officers. I will tell you why they are opened. There is any amount of whiskey smuggled through to the soldiers of the army. There have been boxes come to our Pioneer Corps since I am in it, that had whiskey put into fruit cans and soldered up, so I think you need not send me any. Save them until I get home and I will help you eat them. If you have a mind you may send me a pair of socks by mail—and tell Mr. Buck not to charge too much postage as he did on the hat and gloves. He should not have charged more than 13 cents but I do not care. They suit me first rate and just the fit.

We worked 7 days last week and today is the Sabbath. We had our horses all saddled and mounted to go to work and livery hitched, when Colonel Pierce told us we [would] not work today, so we put our [horses] into the stable again and took our axes and chopped pieces of wood for the old barn, took us probably an hour. So we shaved, we shed and changed shirts, and pants. What a happy day this was. The sun shown warm and bright. The birds were singing their merry glee and almost seemed to say—I wish this cruel war over. Our pickets were silent. Without a shot. Also the canons. The wagon trains were all still and the soldiers were making visits. While I am writing this evening I have not heard a shot. It has seemed more like Sunday today than any other since I am in the army. My mess mates are to bed asleep. Our regiment has moved its quarters farther on our left. I have about 3 miles to go now to see them. I was up to see them this evening before they moved. That memorial had not come. I had some notion to ride up today to see whether it had come. I thought I would wait until next Sunday.

Do you ever hear from Alfreda? I wrote them a letter some weeks ago. They never answered it. I wish you would tell them I shan't write very soon again if they don't answer it. Write when you can and I will do the same. I wrote to you a few days ago. I wanted to know about [where] the Express Office at Meadville was. When we got paid off I intended to express to Meadville. I will have over one hundred dollars coming to me. I received a letter from Tilt [Cyrus Stilton Ellis, Silence's brother]. I also answered it. Let me know in your next letter whether they struck any oil in the McQuiston well. I dreamed of being home the other night. They told me next morning that I said in my sleep to Myron—go and bring Pap kindling from the wood house.

I must close and go to bed. Good night, from well wisher. Write soon.

Samuel K. Miller

February 26, 1865   **Headquarters 9th**
                          Army Corps [Virginia]   **#30**

Dear wife,

Some five or six days has elapsed since I wrote you last. I received a Star [newspaper] from you a day or two ago which was a welcome visitor. I also expected a letter, too, but I have not received one yet. But as this is Sunday evening, I feel somewhat lonesome, sad thoughts. I spend the evening time writing to one that I love.

Today everything is in commotion. The soldiers seem all to feel rejoiced to death to hear of the constant good news that comes to headquarters—of the Rebellion soon coming to a close. It certainly is cheering news indeed to hear of General Sherman's success in the South. There is also a strong rumor that the Rebs are evacuating Petersburgh. If not, there are strong movements going on. They burned their factories last evening about dusk, and a number of other buildings. Grant ordered our Battery men to open a few shots to see whether they were about to evacuate that place but it seems they still occupy the place or at least they replied pretty lively. But deserters say they are evacuating the place just as fast as they possibly can. You can tell the Copperheads that the day is ours, and we do not thank them, either, for their assistance.

The Jonnies come to our lines at an average rate of five hundred per day. Forty six reported here at Headquarters this morning, 35 yesterday. Remember, these only came in on the line of the 9th Corps. On the Army of the James, they number about one hundred per night. They all say the thing is played out. They also say that their leading commanders promised them to not desert until the 4th of March, and then they should go to their homes, but they found out differently by their own good learning. Instead of being sent home they were preparing themselves for a big battle. That is why they desert so. Old Lee is making another move somewhere, but Old Grant is waiting. I would not be at all surprised if we were in Petersburgh next Sunday. That is the supposition by most every one. I hope the thing will soon close.

I can hear something while I am writing that you cannot hear in Crawford County, and that is the little frog's peep. They have peeped for 4 or 5 days. The weather is very warm and pleasant. It did rain yesterday and the day before, but today is as pretty spring weather you ever saw. Tomorrow we expect to be payed off. The paymaster has been paying off for 2 or 3 days, but we only get 4 months pay this time, which will be $64. I shall send it home by express, but I will let you know where and when you will get it.

I saw Mr. Blanchard today. He only works about one hundred rods from where I am. He works at repairing wagons for the army. He was detailed probably a month before I was. He is well and hearty. He says if he ever lives to get home, he and wife are coming to make us a visit. He says his wife writes so much to him about you and me. She thinks you are such a nice woman! I think her head is about right. I got 4 newspapers from David Russle. He also sent me a letter but I never got it. Preacher Rodgers told me he saw a letter for me at the Regiment, but we have some men in our company who have opened a good many letters and destroyed them. There is where that one has gone. It is done by our company clerk.

Give Doctor White my best respects. Tell him for me that the Rebs are a badly whipped nation. We all intend to be home by the 4th of July. Send on your volunteers. There will be no danger of them ever getting into a battle.

The Government has raised the Private's wages to $20 per month. I did not intend to write so much as I have when I commenced but I suppose you would be offended if I wrote only a few lines. I hope you are all well and doing well. I am well also, and hearty. God be with you and family and us all is my wish. From your most kind and affectionate husband,

Samuel K. Miller

March 2, 1865   Headquarters 9th Army Corps [Virginia]   #31

Dear

I received your letter of the 19th on the first day of the present month, which found me in very good health. I was very glad indeed to hear from you all again. Also glad that you and the boys are in good health. I shan't write much in this letter. I wrote in my last letter a few days ago that we should be paid off the next day, but the paymaster did not get around, but tomorrow if the Lord is willing, we shall get our pay. Mr. Rodgers came over today to let us know the regiment would be paid tomorrow. He wanted us to come to the regiment this evening to sign the payroll, but we was out to work and did not get into camp until almost dusk. Again we got our supper and our horses attended to. It was dark and I did not care about going so far alone, for there is danger in traveling about at night for most.

The soldiers have been paid off and there is considerable many been robbed, some hacked down for their money. I did say I would send my money by express but Blanchard thinks we had better send by way of the New Post Office Law. There you can draw your money at Hartstown from Bud—but I will let you know how I will send it and when and how much. I only draw four months pay now. That will amount to $64. I shall send you $60 only—and the four dollars over and above the sixty and what is coming to me from the boys in the company will last me until next pay day, which will probably be in two months.

Again I had a letter from John Miller in Petersburgh [Petersburgh, Ohio, where Samuel lived for many years]. He writes they have another young daughter one month old. Sarah Jane is quite smart again, and the rest of the family are all well. Brother Jacob's [his other brother in Petersburgh, Ohio] folks are all well, also states of the cold weather there and good sleighing. I heard from Brother Jesse's folks. Got one from Charles Carothers. If you write to them please tell them that I have written to them and [they] have never answered. Give them my address. As I said before, I have not much to write so much. I must close. Expecting to hear from you very soon again. Tell Myron that picture has not come yet but I expect it every day and as soon as it comes I will send it. I shall also have my photograph taken on my horse. Just as soon as I get my money. Some day when I feel right I will write to Mother. My love to all and a great share to you. May God be with you and family is my daily prayer. Do not forget me in your thoughts when you lay your weary body upon your bed. No more but from your most kindly husband. Good night, Dearest. Write soon.

Samuel K. Miller

March 11, 1865   Headquarters 9th Army Corps [Virginia]   #32

Dear Wife,

This is Sabbath and I am happy to inform you that I am enjoying good health. I also hope that you and dear children are all well. When I wrote you last I thought we should have made a move, but we still stay in our old place. The prospects are favorable for the 9th Corps to stay here—to hold these lines in front of Petersburgh. Grant has repaired all the front lines, also our rear lines. I will give you a description of our breastworks upon a piece of paper so you can see how the Army of the Potomac lays. Our army is filling up. Every day there are trainloads arriving, filling old regiments, also a number of new regiments. There are three new regiments laying in the woods about one hundred rods in our rear. They are playing some most beautiful pieces on the band. The whole army is in commotion for the last ten days. Grant is making the preparations for a big Battle. All the old soldiers say they never saw such a move as this is going to be. The intention is as near as I can learn, the three corps laying upon our left, the 2nd, 3rd and 6th are to move and form a junction with Sherman. Scofield in the South and Sheridan with his cavalry on the West, Grant with the 9th Corps to hold this place.

We may not move for some time unless the Rebs are whipped and evacuate Petersburgh and Richmond.

I have not had a letter from you for eight or nine days I think. I looked strong for one this evening but was sadly disappointed. So I thought I'd write. I am almost afraid that I will hear in the next letter from you that some of the boys will be drafted, but I hope not, or perhaps they are going to try to fill it by volunteers. Write me the particulars if you have not done so before receiving this. Silence, I send you in this letter two photographs, Grant and Burnsides. I guess you had better give them to Myron. They cost me 30 cents each. I also sent Myron a nice picture paper. Sometime . . . . [the words are too faded to read] . . . also fifty dollars in a letter dated 7th of March. Let me know whether those things came pronto, for I am anxious to hear and have not had my photograph taken. All artists and sutlers [men authorized by the Union Army to sell merchandise to the soldiers] were ordered to the rear last week to City Point. If they had not left I should have had it taken and sent it in this letter.

I went up to my regiment today expecting to get that Memorial but they have not come yet, but expect them every day. I had a letter from Brother Jacob last week. They are all well, but complain dreadfully about hard times and the war. He will pay $100 to clear Bill and Sam from the draft. He may be very glad that he got off for that. It is only fifty dollars for each one. I see today at our regiment that Rodgers has introduced the Morning Star into the company. He gets 8 copies a week. I do love to get a hold of it to read. It does me good—makes me feel just right, but don't neglect sending money for it, for another year.

Silence . . . [the words are too faded to read] . . . today, for it was such a lovely day. The sun shown so beautiful and pleasant. The roads so dusty and nice. The trees coming out green, and everything so lovely that I think about home. I think of you every day and night, but more Saturday night. Silence, I shan't write any more. I may receive a letter from you tomorrow night if so I shall answer it immediately. Give my love to all. Be sure you keep a good share to yourself. I hope you are all well.

Yours truly, forever. Write often.

Samuel K. Miller

[Samuel drew a sketch of the location of 9th Corps and Mounted Pioneers at the bottom of this letter, but it is not included here.]

March 23, 1865   Headquarters 9th Army Corps [Virginia]   #33

Dear wife and children,

I received your letter last evening, Wednesday, dated 12th of the present month which I gladly received. I was also happy to hear that you and little ones were well. It also found me in good health with the exception of a little cold. We have nice weather here. The apple trees are pretty near covered with leaves. They will bloom in a few days. Cherries are in blossom. Everything is growing in spite of the war. Today was the stormiest day I ever saw. You could not see fifty rods for sand. It blew a perfect hurricane all day. We were in the woods cutting and splitting cordoroy timber. We had to stop work for a while on account of so many trees falling. The pines in Virginia are very easily uprooted, the ground being so sandy.

Silence, I suppose sugar making is over any day in Pa. [Pennsylvania]. If you get a chance to buy some at a reasonable price, buy some, but I presume store sugar is about as cheap as home made. You wanted to know when our cow would come in. I drove her to McMaster's I think the last day of June. Bill Andrews went with me and then went home from there to the picnic at the McMichael's. I think you will find it marked on one of the almanacs. She ought to come in the first of next month. Where does those men that have sold their farms intend doing—go west or buy again in the neighborhood? I think the boys had better hold on to their farms for they cannot better themselves, not about there. What did they ever do with Alfreda about her claim? Did she ever send them a deed? If Mother wants to come and live with us, take her. Tell the boys not to run away. Stand the draft and if any of them are drafted to come, there will not be much fighting done.

The Rebs talk strong of making peace. You ought to read the papers and hear what they have to say. There were 40 came to our lines yesterday and today, that is just to our corps. I have prophesied all winter that the war would be closed this spring. I cannot think anything else. I feel like it hard and I can't help it. Did Myron get his picture paper I sent him? And let me know when you get the letter with the fifty dollars. I hope it has gone through, [that it will] be all right.

We have not moved our quarters yet. We may not have to move yet for several months.

How does Mag flourish now a days? Is she cross as ever, and what does she think of her smart brother-in-law? I ought to write to Ab, but I do not like old Mag. Silence, next time you write, let me know how my lumber is, whether it is all stuck up nice yet, and whether you have loaned any tools or whether the neighbors bother you any about working in the shop. I have written you once before about it and you must have forgotten to say anything about it. If it can be done, I would like to have as little done in the shop as possible, for they will spoil my tools and bench, etc. That has bothered me a considerable that my tools will all be carried off and lost. Now remember, let me know in your next letter.

Tell Myron—Mother tells me that little Mead rather bosses you. You must [not?] hurt him when he plays with you. You be good and take good care of him. You must let me know whether he tries to talk any and whether he can jump or not. I sent you two nice photographs. Take good care of them and don't dirty them, and when I come home I will buy a nice photograph album to put them in. I suppose you think that stay away a long time. Just have patience. I will be home pretty soon.

Give my respects to all that inquire about me. I have not written to Mother yet. We have so much to do that I cannot write so many letters. Give my respects to Ellen Johnson. Let me know what John McGregor is doing. Now when I think of it, don't let James McHenry move away and take that calf skin with him. He said he would have it finished by the first of May. Pay him for the tanning of it, for I want a pair of boots made of it, if I live to get home. Write often and give me all the news. I am well and I hope you are well also.

I heard that Loudon is dead, but I am somewhat surprised to hear that Amos and Miss Rudy are going to get married. Did Amos ever pay you what he owes me? If not, dun him for it, for it will come in play to you some day. He can see by looking at the Day Book how much he owes me. He did not settle the books the day I left. I am much obliged to you for sending things in that box if they ever come. Give my love to Mother and you also. [This portion may belong with an earlier letter, one that preceded his getting the box from Hartstown.]

From your most affectionate husband,

Samuel K. Miller

March 27, 1865　　Headquarters 9th Army Corps [Virginia]　#34

Most Affectionate Companion,

I expected to get a letter from you Saturday. Last night Sunday I looked for one and tonight I certainly thought I would get one but was disappointed, so I thought I would write a few lines to let you know that I am well and hearty.

I must also let you know of the great battle fought Saturday morning. It commenced half past four o'clock and lasted until 8—fought 3 ½ [hours]. The Rebs massed there troops the night before unbeknown to us. Their forces numbering about thirty thousand and came through our picket line and cut our in front of our Breastworks and forts and entered Fort Stedman and took all prisoners that were in the fort. Then into the camp and took a great many prisoners before they were awake. Then the Ball opened! By that time the Rebs had captured two of our forts and turned the cannon and commenced shelling us. Those that were engaged in it said they never saw harder fighting. It was hard telling which would come out victorious but at last the Rebs began to waver and in the meantime all the new regiments that have laid all winter in reserve, which will number 6 thousand, made a charge upon the Rebs, which made them skiddadle. We retook our forts and twenty-seven hundred prisoners and killed about three thousand, that is, killed and wounded.

I heard the fight. You could scarcely hear yourself talk for so much firing—both cannon and musketry. The battle was only 1 ½ miles from where we lay. Our regiment was in the fight. Their loss was slight. One man in my company was wounded in the hand. The Rebs calculated to break our lines and destroy our railroad and take City Point, but they failed in doing it. I saw all the prisoners. They were the hardest looking men I ever saw. There were dirty, ragged and a great many without shoes. Oh, such men I never—they are far dirtier looking than the railroad puddies.

It took our troops and the Rebs all day to bury their dead. A great many fell into our hands. Also a great many wounded, which we had to take care of. I saw four flour barrels full of legs and arms taken off by our doctors. Our loss was 5 hundred killed and wounded. It was an awful sight to see those limbs. They were most all Rebel legs and arms. There was a fight on our extreme left the same day. We captured two lines of works and took nine hundred prisoners.

General Sheridan and his entire cavalry force is encamped in the woods in our rear, perhaps one fourth of a mile. Such blowing of bugles you never heard. It makes me feel heart sick. He intends going to form a junction with Sherman. Then you will hear of the greatest battles fought yet, or they will surrender. Charley Carothers thinks it cannot last longer than the middle of May. They are all well and expect us out there this coming fall to make them a visit, or at least they said Mother did not think she would make them a visit until we went along. I would like to go very well myself and see them, but it may be late in the fall when my time is out. I cannot tell when our regiment will be discharged. I think more than likely we will be set free about the first of September. If so, we will have plenty time to go there and make John and Charley a nice visit. Charley talks some of going to Iowa this summer to look him up [a] farm and if he likes the country, he will move there next spring.

Let me know how the draft went. I shan't write any more. I may receive a letter from you in a few days, then I shall write again. I hope you are all well and doing the best you can. Write soon. My prayers for your safety I hope are heard. I expect to hear from you soon. Good night.

From your best earthly friend,

Samuel K. Miller

March 30, 1865   Headquarters 9th Army Corps [Virginia]   #35

Dearest Companion,

Yours of the 20th lays before me and was pleased to hear from you all again and that you were all well. My health still continues good and I am thankful to my God for it. I hope I may have health and strength during my absence. Last night and today all day it has rained steady, which makes it very disagreeable for Grant's army to march and fight. He moved yesterday morning about daylight from here with General Sheridan's and General Craig's entire forces of cavalry besides part of five corps of infantry on our left to make a death blow of the Rebellion. Last night at about half past 10 o'clock, the Rebels massed troops in front of Petersburgh, but was unsuccessful in making the attack. They were received with a rather warm reception from our Batteries, which opened out on them. I never saw such cannonading. You would have thought all the stars in the Heavens were falling. The night was dark and every shell that was thrown looked like a star shooting until it burst, which would make a large flash of light.

You wanted to know of me what I thought of you selling your silk dress. You may do as you please about letting her have it. I don't think you will ever wear it much if you keep it, for it is too light. You can get you another one which I think would suit you much better. I think you are getting all it is worth. You better let her have it and I will buy you one better than that is.

How does Ellen Johnson feel about Charley being drafted? Ben sent me a list of five townships. I see that Andrew I. Galbreath is one on the list. James C. Hart, Bill McLenahan. Oh, but I think that is good for him, the poor, mean Copperhead. It is all good for those Secesh [nickname for those who favored the Secession]. It had ought to of hit George McLenahan and Plum Heagan. They may not see any fighting, for the General and other officers all say it will wind up in about 60 days. Tell

Doctor White for me that I thank him very much for the kindness he has shown towards me and my family. I shall remember him as long as I live, for his kindness and I will make it all right some day. He if a fine man—[even] if he does tell stories about turkey eggs!

I think it will clear off. It has commenced to thunder. We are not at work today. The weather is very warm. We can work all day without our blouses or vests on. I see in the papers that sugar and coffee is on the decline. I presume cotton cloth must be coming down, also. Some of the country merchants will not fare so well as they have done heretofore. I am glad you have your wood procured for the summer. Try and get along the best you can. We will all be home soon. Write often and all the news you know. Let me know what Nate intends to do about the draft. I shall close expecting to hear from you soon again. Give my best respects to White's folks. Tell them the war is progressing fine. Let me know where my letters that I write to you are mailed and how long they are going through. Yours—some of them come in four days and some 7 and 8 days.

I shan't write any more, only if you have an opportunity of buying some apple trees this spring, that is, contract them this spring about as many as I did last spring. Get what you want.

No more at present from your constant well wishing forever,

Samuel K. Miller

April 8, 1865   **Headquarters9ᵗʰArmyCorps,**
                     Nottaway Court House [Virginia]   #36

Dear Wife and Children,

I suppose you would like to hear from me. By this time I suppose you have heard that Petersburgh and Richmond belong to the Yanks, also the South Side Railroad, with forty five thousand prisoners, 8 generals, and driving the Rebs like chaff before the wind. General Lee's army is reduced down to 18,000. The rumor is that Grant gave Lee 12 hours to surrender. If not the Ball goes on. We left our old camp last Monday morning, the 3rd, for the march. We followed the South Side Railroad all the way, a distance of forty four miles. I think we will stop at Burkesville a while, which is the junction of the Danville and Richmond. The darkies are tickled almost to death to see the Yanks.

You cannot expect to hear much from me at this [time], only I am well and hearty. You can hear more at home of this campaign than I can write at present. I am writing this in our wagon. Don't get uneasy about me if you do not hear from me again in two weeks. The thing is going on well. The war is coming to a close very fast. I think by next week we will close the fighting.

My regiment [the 211th Pennsylvania] was in all the fight last Saturday. Sunday my company lost thirteen killed, wounded and missing. Captain Lee was killed, Isaac Graff is missing, also Selkirk Wade. The regiment lost heavy. The fighting was desperate. I saw them fight, make charges. Oh, such a contest I never saw. You will see all the news in the papers. We had pretty hard work on this march. I did not mind that we could ride. I will wait until evening. I may get a letter from you. I hope you are well.

We may all be home before a great while. Don't be alarmed about me, for I think I have a good position. Give my respects to all that may inquire about [me]. I must close for the present, expecting to hear from you soon. The Yanks are all happy, are all eager to close the Rebellion. We live fine. We have hogs, sheep, turkeys, chickens and everything the country affords. Such a destruction of property. Buildings burned and furniture destroyed. I shall tell you all about the raid when I come home.

No more, but I remain yours forever,

Samuel K. Miller

April 11, 1865   Burkesville Junction Headquarters
9th Army Corps   #37

Most dearest ones at home,

The war is over. We are extremely happy. General Lee surrendered with his entire army yesterday the [of this month]. His army has or is being [released] just as fast as they can take the oath and are returning to their homes. The Yanks are the happiest mortals on the face of the globe. To tell the truth we cannot hardly realize that the war is at an end. It does not seem possible. The South Side Railroad is in way of repair. There are three trains of cars in sight from where I am now writing. The road was 3 inches too wide for our cars. One side of the road has been taken up and laid in three inches from Petersburgh to Burkesville a distance of 55 miles since the 3rd of the present month.

This world must be in perfect motion. So happy and rejoiced for myself. I feel happy and have prayed daily for the end, restoration of peace again. I was confident or at least I felt so that it would be over this spring, and my letters will show you that I said so. I can't tell when we will be discharged.

Since I commenced this letter, there is a rumor afloat that our corps is going to start back towards Washington, but where we will stop I cannot tell, but I shall write whenever we stop. Some thinks us one year troops will have to stay our time. Some says we will be discharged. There are thousands that volunteered in 1862, theirs expires the same time ours does. There are thousands that are called veterans that their time will not expire for eighteen months. If the Government can't get enough of men to volunteer into the regular army, then I think the veterans will have to stay their time over. We will know pretty soon who will get going home before their time expires and who will not. For my part, I prefer going home just as soon as they choose to let me.

I have stood the march and war first rate. I had the diarrhea several days of late, but I am well enough now again. My health is also good and I hope you and children are enjoying your selves well. I also hope you are all well. I had a letter from Ben a few days ago. They are all well. Silence, I shan't write much only to let you know where I am, and etc. I shall write every opportunity I have. Yours very respectfully. Write soon. I hope I may get home to help you plant corn. When you see Hiram ask him what I told him about the war coming to a close this spring. I have a ten dollar bill Secesh [Confederate} money but I shan't send it now. It is for Myron.

From your best friend,

Samuel K. Miller

April 16, 1865   Burkville Station [Virginia]
Headquarters 9th Army Corp   #38

Dear ones at home,

This is the Lord's Day in the evening. I thought I would write you a few lines. I am very tired this evening after working hard all day cutting timber for repairing the roads which are in awful condition. The whole army, that is Potomac and James, are on their way towards Richmond and Petersburgh, City Point. Our corps still remains here and along the South Side Railroad from this place to Petersburgh. I cannot tell you how long we may stay here, but I rather think not very [much] longer.

I received your letters dated 4th and 5th, I think on Friday last, which found me well and hearty. I was also very glad to hear from you all and your good health. I got the socks you sent me. I want you to [be] careful not to work too hard or undertake to make garden. Hire someone to spade the ground and fix up the beds, for you cannot do it all.

I suppose you will hear of the murder of Lincoln before this reaches you and all the particulars, also about the assassination of Secretary Steward. I have not heard anything for 10 years that has hurt my feelings so much as the murder of those men, but I presume it was the Lord's will they should die. He was killed by a confounded Rebel which I presume in all probability was bribed to do the deed. Oh, what a wicked man he must be. Hanging is too good for him. The soldiers all swear a vengeance against the Rebs. The Rebs are all that Lee surrendered running about at large. I can [see] hundreds of them every day, mostly dirty, thieving set of fellows, but that are watched very closely by our troops so they do not do any mischief to the Railroads.

I suppose there were some cannonading in Hartstown and other places when they got the news that Lee had surrendered his army. I heard today that Joe Johnson had surrendered his army, but it is not official but he will before a great while. I hope he will [surrender] so as we can get home by harvest.

Silence, I can't write much for I have no place to write, only on the ground. You can hear all the war news at home. Thank God the war is about to come to a close. That we men that have friends dear to us may be spared to return home to them where we may enjoy a Christian life with those that have been pious and said and done all to persuade them to share an interest in the love of Christ. I still am determined to be a Christian and pray to my God every day for the conversion of my soul.

Silence, I will close expecting to see you all soon. I also expect to hear from you. I hope you are well. I am well. Write often. I will do the best I can under the circumstances I am placed at the present time. Good night. May the angels guard you in your slumbers.

Yours forever truly,

Samuel K. Miller

April 25, 1865   City Point, Virginia
9th Army Corps U.S. Christian
Commission [letter heading]   #39

I again take the opportunity of writing a few lines stating of my health is very good. Also to let you know that I received your letter of the 9th. You know that I received your letter of the 9th of the present month some four or five days since, which I had not time to answer on account of the march. We landed here a couple days ago, and are waiting hourly for transportation for Washington. My regiment [211th Pennsylvania] is at Washington now. What the Government intends doing with us, we have not yet learned. There are rumors in circulation that the 9th Corps is to be disbanded and sent home for sixty days. If not wanted in that time, to be discharged and sent home. Some say we are going to Texas and others say we are going to North Carolina.

Our corps is all at Washington but one division and that is here waiting for boats. They are taking all their wagon trains, horses, mules and artillery and everything. I only hope we will be sent home, for I am sick and tired of soldiering. We have nothing to do here, only take care of our horses and eat and lay around in our tents. Mercy, but it is hot today. I have nothing on me but pants and a shirt. I hope you and babies are well and try and get along first rate. I must close, expecting to hear from you soon. I shall write again when I get to Washington, which will be probably the last of this week. Take care of yourself.

Your husband very truly. Don't think hard for not writing more.

Samuel K. Miller

April 30, 1865   Headquarters 9th Army Corps,
                           Alexandria, Virginia   #40

Dear Wife,

We are laying one mile and a half from Alexandria. We arrived here yesterday morning about sunrise. My regiment is in sight from where we lay. They are all in good spirits of a speedy discharge. I think myself that we will be sent to our respective states this week. We may not get home for two weeks or not until the first of June. The war is over. Johnson has surrendered his army to Sherman. Kirby Smith has surrendered also. The War Department has stopped the purchase of all supplies, also the buying of horses, mules, cattle, only for the regular army. I have not been to Washington, yet I would like to go to see the boys, but I presume that we will stop there long enough so I can go to see them.

I have not had a letter from you for about 10 or 12 days. The reason why was that our squad was left at the point with our stock and wagon train waiting for transportation and not knowing what moment there would [be] a boat, so our mail was kept at Washington. I presume we will get it tomorrow. I am well and fat and hearty and I hope with patience to see you all soon. I hope you and children are all well. I hope to be home to hoe my potatoes and corn this spring. I pray that God may spare my health and life.

I thank God that He has been merciful in sparing my life to this point and hope He will in the future.

Write soon direct as usual, until further orders.

Your kind husband,

Samuel K. Miller

[An additional part of letter, not sure which date.]

You said you thought the war was about over. Yes, the great conflict has come to a close and our country is once more restored to peace and happiness, and the fiendish enemy are getting their just dues. Wherever there are any, they are shot down like brutes in the forest. A man is not allowed to speak any disloyal sentiments whatever. If he does, he is shot or ways seriously punished, which is just right. George McLenahan and some others that are rank Sesesh would not fare very well here if they talk as they did when I was home.

I presume that you have heard that Booth has been captured and shot. His body no one knows where it is. The paper stated it was thrown into the bottom of the Potomac River. We also heard that Jeff Davis is killed. He was killed, if true, by his own men. He well deserved killing or something as bad. The Government is discharging District troops, now all Pennsylvania troops will be sent to their respective states, there to be discharged as fast as possible in order to reduce the recent expenses to one fourth by the first of June.

You need not look for me until you see [me], for I am not able to tell you when I shall be home, but sometime between now and the first of June if the Lord is willing. We cannot say we will do so, unless the Lord lets us. Some of the boys swear and curse what they are going to do when they get home. All these things. Oh, I would not curse and swear as they do, and curse their Maker every word they utter for the whole world. It makes the cold chills run all over me.

I have no faults to find with you about the pigs. Seven dollars is a big price for two pigs but you did the best you could. I presume 7 dollars would not buy the pork we should use in the family in the winter. You have done exceedingly well. I hope you and me may live to be one [hundred] years old.

May 2, 1865   **Headquarters 9ᵗʰ Army Corp,**
                         Alexandria, Virginia   **#41**

Dear folks at home,

I received your letter of the 19ᵗʰ, which day it was mailed. You had no
date to it, but I was very glad to hear from you that you are all well and
hearty. We moved our camp yesterday morning to a government stable
where we have a good place for our horses. Where we first encamped
was down the Potomac River about one and a half miles below the
city of Alexandria and now we lay off the road between this place and
Washington, perhaps six miles from Washington.

I have not been down to see the boys. If I can get a pass, I shall go. I
think Enoch is very green and foolish to have his wife to go to such a
place when his time is so near out, just as though she could not stand
it four months longer. You know what I mean. She will hear some nice
conversation among the soldiers.

Silence, I will close, expecting to hear from you soon and publications.
See you all soon

where we may enjoy the balance of our days in happiness.

Yours very truly,

Direct as usual.

Samuel K. Miller

I shan't write long letters any more for I can tell you far more than I can
write.

May 4, 1865   **Headquarters 9ᵗʰ Army Corps,**
                         Alexandria, Virginia   **#42**

Beloved ones at home.

I received a letter dated 25 April, also one from C. Carothers last evening. You may be advised I was glad to hear from you all again. Charles is well. I am well, also, and hearty, but most dreadfully tanned, almost as dark as a mulatto, but I need not care, it only goes skin deep. I was just taking a walk through the city of Alexandria. It is a very pleasant city. The buildings look as though they had been built a great many years ago and in a state of dilapidation. The soldier boys monopolize the streets. A young man by the name of Brown from the State of New York, a man in our squad of good morals and habits, and myself were together in a news depot looking at some photographs and amongst the rest I saw two that were very nice and very affecting to me. [One] was a young man going to the army with a wife and two small children and probably the same age as our two. His farewell adieu, the final embraces, and at the end of three years his return home, which is very affecting, his welcome return to his warmest bosom friend on earth.

No one can appreciate the feeling that exists within his heart toward those at home until he has had the experience. I have been from home three years at a time. I never saw any relatives left behind me that was so fascinating to me as my loved companion and little ones that inhabit our little dwelling at home. I hope ere [before] the rising of a great many suns to be in their midst, enjoying the comforts of society and the privileges of mingling our feeble prayers with those that are true Christians. I feel happy to think the war is at a close. I also feel sad and shed tears to read about those poor rebels and blacks—how rejoiced they are to be liberated from bondage. The playing of a band of musicians makes me shed tears. It seems that my heart is completely broken. The boys all say I am so quiet. I cannot help it. I feel so. May it be the Lord's will that we may all safely return to our respective homes where we may forever worship Him that is ever watchful over us. Silence, don't neglect to pray for me, for I know you are a Christian and how wicked I have been that I was not one also, but if God spares my life I shall be one, too. I feel happy all the time but fear I am still in darkness.

Friday morning [the] 5th. This morning is warm but has the appearance of rain. We still have our horses to take care of. We may have to turn them over in a few days and we may stay with them until our regiment is sent home. Then, of course, we shall have to go along. We have nothing to do at all, only take care of our horses and eat, but lying on the ground uses me up. It gives me the back ache some nights, that in the morning I can scarcely get up. The time is not far hence when this lying upon the ground will be over. We can get anything to eat and drink we want by paying for it. Milk for 10 cents a quart, and butter 20 cents per pound. We don't draw hardtack anymore, nothing but soft bread. If a man bought everything you see you might spend all your money in a little while.

I have written three letters since we came to Alexandria, and received two from you and one from Charles. Sherman's army is coming to Alexandria, then the two armies are to have a grand review. The War Department has ordered six hundred thousand discharges printed immediately. All citizen enlistees [?] are discharged. It may take to the first of June before they get entirely through discharging all the armies. You can see by reading the papers what the War Department is doing.

I have nothing more to write, only I am well and hope are all are well, also. Give my respects to White's folks and to all that may inquire about me. Take a good share of my love to yourself. Tell Myron to have patience and I will be home soon. Did he ever get them photographs I sent him?

Write often. A letter comes through in two days. I could write all day, but will tell you all when I see you.

Samuel K. Miller

May 11, 1865   **Headquarters 9th Army Corps,**
                       Alexandria, Va.   **#43**

Dear Wife,

Yours of the 7th came duly to hand and [it] is now before me. I was glad to hear from you, also that you were well. As regards my own health is very good, and I am thankful to God for it. You remarked that you were rejoiced to hear that I soon would reoccupy my place again at our little home. I hope the time may not be far distant when we may all once meet here on Earth.

I was down to Washington today with the sergeant and one of the boys out [of] the Pioneer Corps with a team for a few things for Lieutenant Colonel Pierce, but did not have time to go to see the boys. I was within a short distance of the White House, too, but could not leave to see them. Everything seems to move off briskly.

I had a letter from Enoch last Monday. He stated that Mary I. had gone home. She was there eight days. I do not consider it a suitable place for a woman, for there are so many remarks made by the soldiers that have been deprived of female society so long. I should not have you come to see me for all that I am worth, but I presume it suits them, so I have nothing more to say upon the subject.

Jacob's folks need not be uneasy about me, for I wrote to them last. I also stated that Grant intended to change Lee's works this spring. He has done it, and was successful—and the war is over.

Oh, how strange it seems to hear no cannon or musketry any more. It hardly seems possible that the Rebellion is crushed. Your Uncle Springer I do not remember of ever hearing you say anything about them. If you have, I have forgotten all about it. You can give them my best respects. I hope to see them before they return home or as soon as Charles Miller. The talk is now [that] the Ninth Corps will be one of the first corps discharged. We are all getting tired to death [of] laying about doing nothing. Not enough to digest our food. We have turned in our horses and all our equipment, so you see we have not even our horses to take care of. I wish they would send us [to] our regiments. There we would have [a] little drilling to do, but I will not find any fault, only time seems long. I want you to write often if it is not more than 10 lines. This letter came through in two days. It was mailed the 9th, and arrived here the 11th at four o'clock. Tell Silence I will bring her a nice album or I can send her one by mail. Tell Myron I will bring him a drum. I would send it by mail, but I think Uncle Sam would be obliged to furnish and extra mail bag. Milo, I will have to bring him something nice, too.

It has been very wet here for several days. We are having a very heavy thunder shower and a few hail. I saw green peas, lettuce, radishes, onions _____ a great many _____-market at Alexandria. I have a letter that I will send you in this letter, written by a Southern Lady at Charleston, South Carolina, which is good. I cut it out of a Washington Chronicle.

Oh, I sent my overcoat home by express to Evansburgh in a box with Osker See and J. B. Miller. If you or any [of] our folks are up that way, call and get it. You will find the coat at Mrs. See. I did not mark my coat but I will tell you how you will know it. There is a pocket in the left skirt at the waist on the outside with those gloves in it you sent me—also a breast pocket on the inside of the right breast. The coat looks clean and is made of felt cloth, but we may get home before the box.

I shan't write any more. Expecting to hear from you again very soon. Do not put off writing so long. It was nine days between your two last letters. I wish you health and all the good wishes you want.

Samuel K. Miller

May 14, 1865   **Alexandria, Virginia (Confidential)   #44**

Direct as usual until further orders. Please don't read this or any of my letters to any one.

Dear wife and children,

Your letter of the 10th is before me, which came to hand the 13th. I was somewhat surprised to get one so soon. I never got them but once a week, but to tell you the truth, it does me good to hear from you. If it was not for time and expense, I would not care if I could get a letter every day, but I shan't ask that of you for I know you have plenty to do to take care of the house work and children, and other chores that rest upon you, without turning your whole attention to writing. So I get one a week, that is all I shall ask of you.

If God is willing, I hope to be home by the first of June. There will be a general review of the whole army at Washington, Just as soon as Sherman's troops reach this point, that will be probably next Wednesday, the 17th, which will take two or three days. Then, the War Department intends to pay the army and discharge them as fast as they can. There is a rumor afloat that all cavalry men—that their time expires by the first of October—to be discharged immediately. There are troops being discharged now every day, such as prisoners and hospital bombers, etc.

Enoch was up yesterday to see me. He is well and looks well enough. He said that he was unwell last week several days. I supposed he had slept rather close to Mary Jane. He said it only cost him $2.50 per day for him and her while she stayed. That is all well enough. Money is plenty and who cares for expenses, I suppose they think. Enoch told me it was Mrs. Lincoln wish to have the boys discharged when she left Washington. She intends moving out next Wednesday for Springfield, Illinois.

Ben and Martin are both well. I promised Enoch to go and see them this week, but I do not know whether I can go or not. We have beautiful weather now, warm and pleasant. Oh, how I would love to be home to work about and fix up things. I presume some things need fixing by this time, not blaming you at all for letting them get in that way. The soldiers are all complaining about lying around. They say—why don't the government discharge us and send us home? Then they will curse and swear and get drunk. There is nothing too bad for them to say or do. They don't even thank their Heavenly Father for the preservation of their wicked souls to the present time. No, they don't think the Lord has any control over them. Oh, what a wicked people. It seems as though they disregarded God and man. God is a merciful God, as one have been in this war would have been cut down for their wickedness, which they have committed in using profane language. I would not dare to attempt the like. I think sometimes when I read God's word and pray to him for forgiveness and thank Him for health and strength, I fall short of doing my duty.

Sabbath morning. Today's papers have the glorious news of the capture of old Jeff Davis and his whole gang. He was captured at Irwinsville, Georgia. In all probability he will be hung by the neck. I think he deserves a severe punishment for he has been the great cause of all this dreadful carnage in our country and so much loss of blood and the cause of a many fatherless child, also caused a many a widow. By reading the newspapers, you can see the particulars of Jeff's capture and what they intend doing with the old chap. Let me know in your next letter how the Copperheads seem to feel about the assassination of President Lincoln. The Copperheads here dare not chirp or say anything disloyal in regard to it.

I am well and hearty and hope this may reach you in safety and find you all in health and spirits. I also hope I may soon be released from bondage and all go home. Give my best respects to all that inquire about me. Be sure to keep a good share to yourself. Tell Myron the drum must [be] coming. From your husband forever. Write often.

Samuel K. Miller

May 21, 1865   Alexandria, Virginia   #45

Dear Silence,

Yours of the 18th is before me, which I received this afternoon. I was much pleased to hear from you also that you and babes were well. I am well as common, or at least so as to make way with my rations. Next Tuesday and Wednesday is set apart for the final review, 23rd and 24th. The armies are to march in company front up Pennsylvania Avenue from the Capitol to the White House, thence to their respective camps again in light marching order without knapsacks. Immediately after the review we will return to our states to be discharged, which will probably take a week or ten days, not more than that as the furtherest.

I cannot tell you positively when I will be home. I will tell you more when we get to Camp Reynolds. I don't think I will be in the review unless we are sent to our regiments tomorrow or Monday. I will know in a day or two what they will do with us. You need not look for me until you hear me shut the gate and whistle. I may be home in 10 days and I may not get home for two weeks. You may be assured that I will come just as soon as Uncle can furnish me with transportation. I am just as anxious to get home as you are to have me come home. I also hope the Lord willing to permit [me] to go home.

There were a few days this week that was very warm but for the last three days it has rained, which has cooled the air. I am afraid it will rain upon the days of review, if so, it will make it disagreeable under foot and overhead both.

Silence, I want you to write again to me, and direct to the Regiment S. K. Miller, Company A, 211th Pa V, Washington, D. C. I think that is the way you directed them to me before I was detailed. Write as soon as you get this—if it is not more than 10 lines. I will close expecting to hear from you soon. I expect too, when I get home to get a sweet kiss or have they soured. I think you might [have] told me that last question I asked, but never mind, you will tell me when I get home.

From your well wisher and forever yours,

Very truly,

Samuel K. Miller

May 24, 1865   **Alexandria, Virginia**   **#46**

Dear ones at home,

Yours of the 19th lays before me on the ground, or rather on the bed, which I read this morning. I am pleased to hear from you all again that you were well. I am as well as usual but tired almost to death waiting for glorious news to go home. I was up to my regiment today. They told me there that they thought we would start for home on Friday or Saturday for certain. I think tomorrow I will be sent to my regiment. I hope at least. The boys are all crazy to get home to see their wives and babies—like myself—my company are most all married persons.

I was not up to Washington to see the review. I need not tell you for why. You know that I do not care much for such things. You said Hiram wished me to bring him a couple of soldiers blankets. I will if I can. New ones will cost him five dollars each. I always intended to take two or three home for myself, providing I can get them by getting them for nothing. I think there will be lots of such chances at Camp Reynolds, or if I can buy them for fifty cents or a dollar apiece I will bring some home. It will not take more than three for a load. They are awfully heavy. Tell him I will accommodate him if I can.

Silence, as I said in my last letter to you, I cannot set no time when I shall be home. You may look for me just a little about the 3rd of June, but not too much for fear you may be disappointed. John Henry told me today that he saw Dr. Gibson at Washington, also Thero Moats and James J. Groop from Jamestown.

Silence, you are a bully old gal. You may have a nice pair of booties made of that calf skin. I will also bring you a nice present. Tell Myron that drum must come. Be a nice boy and I will fetch some pretty things. I do not know whether it is much use to write any more at present. I shall write to you as often as I can and let you know as near as I can when you may watch for me. If you feel disposed to answer this, direct (it) to the Regiment as you did when I first came out, only you need not direct to the captain as you did before, for Lee is dead—direct to the regiment. My respects to all and my love to you.

From your affectionate husband,

Samuel K. Miller

Appendix C

Samples of Samuel K. Miller's handwritten letters

al Parks of the Ninth army corps of
mac to the Mounted Pioneer corps
I plain to You as well as I can what we
do. In the first place. We have horses
where ever we go if not more then
— there are 25 men in the company
so there is any bridge to build or
we have it to do = also go with the
ion train help them through fix
&c we carry no gun or arms of any
— we will not be placed in any danger
amy—the work is middling hard but
easier work if a man is in safety this
went or take for one Year or more
ll pleased with my Position the
hey detaild me was they wanted men
a study and did not drunk &c —
finished our cabin are into it this
is the first night. I would have answ
better before but had no chance for th
to were so crouded that I could not

ten days ago I shall write to You often now
for when our days work is done we have no
more to do until next day we never get up
until 7 Oclock we also have a man to do our
cooking all we do is to go to the cook shanty
and get our plates + tin cups get our grub +
then go to our tents eat and carry our dishes
back and they are all washed and kept there
until the next meal we get soft bread every
day roast beef sometimes fryed pork also baked
beans—I have eat my molasses + one can of
apple butter my butter what I kept is done but
I have 4 lbs loaned that I shall get back again
in a few days the beauty of belonging to this
Pioneer corps is You have no luggage to carry
it is all hauled by our waggons that are in the
corps I was chosen as a axman some carry pick
some spades &c Jesse writes that he has bought
a farm on the road between Mercer
+ Georgetown he also gets the post office
I have not heard from any of the rest of the

I will send You my likeness Just as soon
as I get my pay if that does not suit You
I will bring Your present when I come —

Direct S. K. Miller
Mounted Pioneer, Head quarters 9th Army
Corps Washington D. C.

     Samuel K. Miller

write soon as You Recd this So good
buy for the Present.

     From Your husband &c

the News came to head quarters
that Sherman has taken Charleston
but thought doubtfull. What does
George Mcgranahan think about the
war now also about the draft. I can
tell You the reason You aid not get
more wood cut—because You are a
abolishenist wife: What do they think now
about me going to the army—I would like
to talk to some of them Coppyheads I think
I could tell them some things that would not
set very well on their stomacks. Silence here
do Yout get along Sleeping alone—dont You
wish You me some nights—with my cold
feet = (nonecence) I am well I hope You are
to—Kiss the Babies for me

— January 8th 1865
Head quarters army of the Potomac
Dear Wife

     I was Just down to my Regt a distance of
a mile. Expecting a letter from You I am very happy
to say I was not disappointed as You said You
were Oh how I was pleased to hear that You were
all well again. for I was very uneasy about myson
not getting along I am also happy to say the Lord
is blessing one with good Health. I thank him for
it daily. I pray that he may watch + protect all
my lifetime. Well I Just finished my dinner +
watered my horse so I will endeavor to scrible
a few more lines to You I have not much news
to write to day I wrote You a letter last Sabbath
and one a few days previous to that I am sorry
that You did not git more wood cut the day of
Your frolick—after going to so much bother in
prepareing for it. the Next one You make dont
calculate it so far ahead make it when the snow
is good or the weather is nice but however I
suppose You done the best You could I

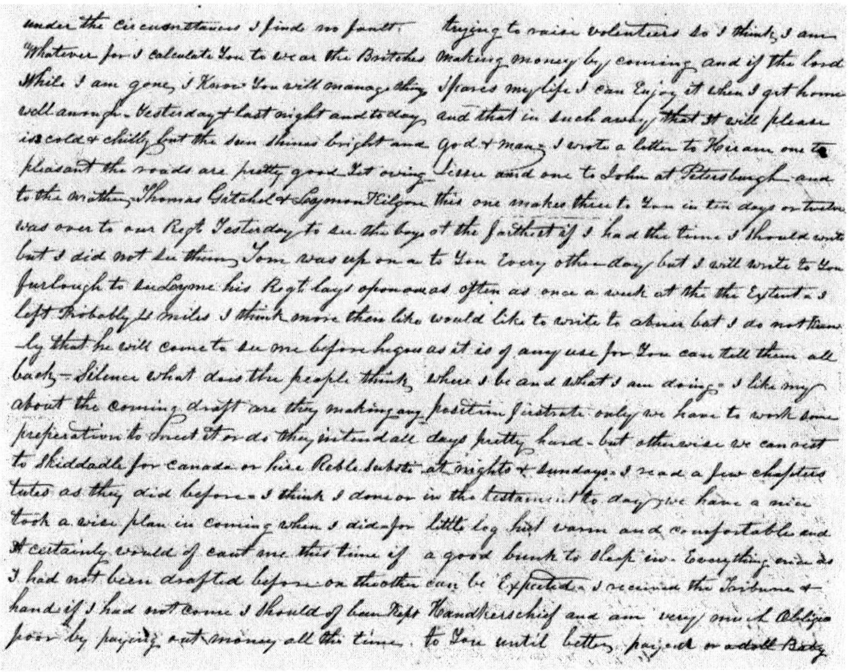

under the Circumstances I find no fault
Whatever for I calculate You to wear the Britches
While I am gone, I Know You will manage things
well enough. Yesterday & last night and today
is cold & chilly but the sun shines bright and
pleasant the roads are pretty good Yet owing
to the weather Thomas Getchel & Seymon Kilgore
was over to our Regt Yesterday to see the boys
but I did not see them Tom was up on a
furlough to see Wayne his Regt lays op on a
left probably 4 miles I think more then like
-ly that he will come to see me before he goes
back – Silence what does the people think
about the coming draft are they making any
preperation to meet it or do they intend all
to Skiddadle for canada or hire Reble substi
tutes as they did before – I think I done or
took a wise plan in coming when I did for
it certainly would of caught me this time if
I had not been drafted before on the other
hand if I had not come I should of been kept
poor by paying out money all the time.

trying to raise volunteers so I think I am
making money by coming and if the lord
spares my life I can Enjoy it when I get home
and that in such a way that it will please
God & man. I wrote a letter to Hiram one to
Jesse and one to John at Petersburgh and
this one makes three to You in ten days or twelve
at the furthest if I had the time I should write
to You Every other day but I will write to You
as often as once a week at the the Extent – I
would like to write to others but I do not know
as it is of any use for You can tell them all
where I be and what I am doing – I like my
position first rate only we have to work some
days pretty hard – but otherwise we can rest
at nights & Sundays. I read a few chapters
in the testament to day we have a nice
little log hut warm and comfortable and
a good bunk to sleep in – Everything o.k. as
can be Expected – I received the Tribune &
Handkerchief and am very much Obliged
to You until better paid or a doll Body

Bibliography

Books:

Barclay, William. *The Letter to the Romans*. Westminster: John Knox Press. 2002.

Bates, Samuel P. *History of the Pennsylvania Volunteers 1861-65*. Vol. 4. Harrisburg, Pennsylvania: B. Singerly, State Printer, 1869-1871.

Bates, Samuel P., Brown, R. C., Mansfield, J. G, *History of Crawford County, Pennsylvania*. 2 vols. Chicago: Warner, Beers & Company, 1885.

Brawley, Benjamin. *"Lorenzo Dow,"* The Journal of Negro History, vol. 1, no. 3. Lancaster, Pennsylvania: The Association of the Study of Negro Life and History, Inc. 1916.

McIvigan, John R. *The War Against Proslavery Religion: Abolitionism and the Northern Churches, 1830-1865*. Ithaca: Cornell University Press,. September 2009.

Miller, Milo H. *A History and Genealogy of the John Ellis Family, 1797-1935*. Bedford, Ohio: Miller Printing Company, 1935.

Miller, Milo H. *A History and Genealogy of the Miller Family 1725-1933*. Bedford, Ohio: Miller Printing Company, 1933.

Rogers, Fred. *The World According to Mister Rogers: Important Things To Remember*. New York: Hyperion, 2003.

Tick, Edward. *War and the Soul: Healing our Nation's Veterans from Post-traumatic Stress Disorder.* Wheaton, Illinois: Quest Books, Theosophical Publishing Company, 2005.

Trudeau, Noah Andre. *Petersburg, Virginia June 1864-April 1865.* Baton Rouge: Little Brown & Company, 1991.

Wagner, Margaret E., Gallagher, Gary W., Finkelman, Phil, Editors. *The Library of Congress Civil War Desk Reference.* New York: Simon & Schuster. Paperbacks. 2002

Magazines and Journals:

Perri, Timothy J. "The Economics of US Civil War Conscriptions." *American Law and Economics Review* 10:2 (2008): 424-453. Web. 23 Feb. 2011.

Newspapers:

"Crawford Democrat." Meadville, Pennsylvania. 1840-1884. On film at the Crawford County Historical Society, Meadville, Pennsylvania.

Internet Sources:

"About Hillsdale." *Hillsdale College.* Web. 20 Feb. 2011.

   http://www.hillsdale.edu

"A Union Soldier's Uniform from the Civil War, around 1865." *Memorial Hall* Museum and Library, American Centuries: History and Art from New England.

   http://americancenturies.mass.edu/activities/dressup/notflash/civil_war_soldier.html

"Copperheads." *Dictionary of American History, 2003. Encyclopedia. com.* Web. 28 Feb, 2011.

   http://www.encyclopedia.com/doc/1G2-3401801035.html

Hayton, Daris. "Wright's Indian Vegetable Pills." *PACHSmorgabord, Philadelphia Area Center for History of Science.* October 18, 2009. Web. 24 Feb. 2011.

   http://www.pachs.net/blogs/comment/wrights_indian_vegetable_pills/

Sandow, Robert M. *"Home Front,"* 150 Pennsylvania Civil War, 2011. Web. 28 Feb, 2011.

   http://www.pacivilwar150.com/understand/pennsylvania.aspx

Sandow, Robert M. *"Pennsylvania's Role,"* 150 Pennsylvania Civil War, 2011. Web. 28 Feb. 2011.

   Http://www.pacivilwar150.com/understand/pennsylvania.aspx

Wentworth, Ed. "Industrial Era: The Morning Star." Seacoast New Hampshire, 1998. Web. 28 Feb. 2011.

   http://www.SeacoastNH.com

Another excellent Internet site for a description of the life of the Civil War solder is:

Heiser, John. "The Civil War Soldier: What was life as a soldier like in 1863?" *Gettysburg National Military Park, United States Department of the Interior, National Park Service.* 1 May, 1998. Web. 27 Feb. 2011.

   http://www.nps.gov/archive/gett/soldierlife/cwarmy.htm

Edwards Brothers,Inc!
Thorofare, NJ 08086
13 April, 2011
BA2011103